Science Chatterbox
Yrs 5/6

Chris Jones

Key Facts
Publications

Published by
Key Facts Publications,
West Ferry Road
Canary Wharf, London E14

Copyright © Chris Jones 2008

Key Facts Publications books are protected by international copyright
laws. All rights reserved. The copyright of all materials in this book,
except where otherwise stated, remains the property of the publisher
and the author. No part of this publication may be reproduced, stored
in a retrieval system, or transmitted in any form or by any means,
for whatever purpose, without the written permission of
Key Facts Publications.

Photocopying is allowed within the purchasing institution,
of all Chatterbox worksheets in this publication.

ISBN   978-0-9561456-0-4

Author - Chris Jones

Editors - Carrie Lee, Jill Sexton

Photography and Logo - Peter Jones

Graphic Design - Muriel Moukawem

This book is dedicated to mum
who is quite simply, the best, and
always supports me, whatever I do.

Acknowledgements

Special thanks go to Carrie Lee, who suggested writing this book in the first place. Also to Jill Sexton, Peter Jones, Sathi Singh, Olga Venzhina, Mike Scantlin and Leigh Scantlin, for their parts in helping to make this book actually happen. I would like to extend my gratitude to all my other friends and family, who have offered their encouragement and best wishes during the whole process.

Finally, a big thank you to the head, Mark Macauley, the rest of the staff, the parents and especially to the wonderful children of St Joseph's RC Primary School in Bermondsey, where I spent eleven happy and rewarding years.

Contents

Introduction

Science Chatterboxes are an innovative new resource that will inspire and motivate the science teaching and learning in your class. They are an excellent way to raise standards throughout the whole of KS2 and if used regularly, will impact on the end of Key Stage 2 science SAT's results.

Science Chatterboxes comprehensively cover, in 'bite sized' chunks, all the key aspects of scientific knowledge and understanding required for KS2, with a particular emphasis on the important scientific vocabulary - enabling children to articulate themselves confidently. They serve as a valuable resource of over 1000 questions, all linked to the QCA units of work and levelled from 3-5 to cater for every ability, including your gifted and talented.

They are based on the timeless children's playground game, commonly known as 'Fortune Tellers' - (there's many regional variations!) – but adapted to make learning fun and exciting. More importantly, they make perfect VAK activities and will engage children from all learning styles; visual, auditory and kinaesthetic.

Chatterboxes also encourage and promote Personalised Learning by allowing the children to adapt, annotate and illustrate - encouraging them to become proactive, self-motivated learners and to make the science knowledge their own.

This is a resource for both teachers and children to adapt and make their own. After all, that's what we do best!!

Teaching and Learning Benefits

Science Chatterboxes are a fun way of learning, enjoyed by all children. They have many benefits, all helping to create a positive learning experience.

Promote Personalised Learning

Children should be encouraged to annotate or illustrate the answers, using the blank spaces in the Chatterbox. This gives the children ownership of the learning, increasing their retention.

Ideal VAK Activity

Visual: Important scientific vocabulary, definitions and statements are highlighted by means of different font styles and sizes, in order to stand out. It is important that children are encouraged to add colour and illustrations to the sheets - to enhance their visual learning.

Audio: Children love to ask each other questions, listening intently to their friends' responses - this repetition of the questions and responses, helps in reinforcing the important scientific vocabulary and definitions.

Kinaesthetic: The Chatterbox is particularly suited for those kinaesthetic learners who often, 'find it hard to remain on task'. The whole nature of the Chatterboxes involves both physical and mental participation at a variety of levels; from cutting, folding, annotating and holding, to asking questions and checking the answers. Furthermore, no writing is involved and children do not always have to sit round a table!

Differentiation

All the Chatterbox sheets are levelled 3-5, helping to differentiate for all abilities, including your gifted and talented.

Activity Ideas

Science Chatterboxes follow and fully support the KS2 QCA Units of Study (they also complement all other primary science schemes of work). The worksheets are fully differentiated and can be used in pairs, small groups or the whole class.

There are many ways for using this resource, here are just a few suggestions:

- **Within Science Lessons**

    Starter: Just as literacy and numeracy lessons begin with a 10 minute word or mental starter, try doing the same for science using the Chatterboxes.

    Investigations: Try using one of the questions as a starting point for an investigation.

    Brainbreaks: Chatterboxes could be used as an ideal 'brainbreak' activity within a lesson.

    Reinforce Current Learning: Use at an appropriate time during the lesson to reinforce current learning or to introduce new ideas/concepts.

    Plenary: Use during the plenary - teacher holds the Chatterbox and asks the questions.

- **Assessment for Learning**: Blank out the questions or answers before photo-copying - children write an appropriate entry. How well the children are able to articulate their responses, provides a useful formative assessment tool. Alternatively, children could show their responses using a whiteboard.

- **Customise Your Own**: Use the blank format to create your own customised chatterbox. Using the blank format, children could make their own - to help consolidate their learning and understanding.

- **SAT's Revision**: Could be used during SAT's revision, an ideal short activity for use during booster revision classes.

- Chatterboxes are a popular **homework** activity!

Instructions for Making

1. Cut out the square Chatterbox.

2. Fold and unfold the Chatterbox, along all four lines of symmetry. The creases will form a 'star' in the centre of the sheet.

3. Place Chatterbox on a flat surface, the blank side facing up. Fold each corner into the centre of the 'star'.

4. Turn the Chatterbox over. Fold each corner into the centre of the 'star'.

5. Fold the Chatterbox in half - so facing outwards, are four square flaps.

6. Insert your thumbs and index fingers under the flaps. As you pinch your fingers together, the Chatterbox will take shape.

7. Now Colour, illustrate and personalise your chatterbox!

Several other sets of instructions can be found on the internet, including pictures, diagrams and movie clips, as well as written text.

Instructions for Using Chatterboxes

There is no single 'set in stone' set of instructions, here is one suggestion.

1. Hold the Chatterbox and ask your partner to, 'select one of the four science words'.

2. Spell the word out aloud, opening/shutting the Chatterbox at the same time.

3. Ask your partner to 'select a number from 1-4 or 5-8' depending which half is open.

4. Repeat the counting process.

5. Ask your partner to 'select a number from 1-4 or 5-8' - this time, read out the corresponding question.

6. The correct response is revealed by lifting the flap.

DIET

Keeping Healthy Unit 5A

1 On a poster, it said 'eat different kinds of food, and exercise regularly'. What was it about?

2 What's the name of the red liquid that circulates around the body?

Science Chatterbox 1

VARIETY

5 What does pulse rate measure?

staying healthy

how **fast** your **heart** is beating

blood

the **HEART**

Which organ pumps blood around the body?

What is the **heart made from**?

muscle (protein)

exercise and **movement**

watching TV - all the rest are healthy activities

About **74 – 78** **beats** per minute

How **fast** is the **average** persons 'resting pulse rate'?

© Chris Jones 2008

8

HEALTHY

4 Carbohydrates are a good food for **which kind of activity**?

3 Which is the **odd one out**: running, swimming, watching TV, cycling?

7

BALANCED

© Chris Jones 2008

Unit 5A

Keeping Healthy

Chatterbox 2   Level 3

VITAMINS

Keeping Healthy

Unit 5A

1 The repeated movements that keep the heart, muscles & joints in good working order are?

2 Helpful drugs are called?

FRUIT

Science Chatterbox 2

What is the heart's main function?

5 Chemical substances which have an effect on the body are called ....?

exercise

drugs

medicines

the heart pumps blood around the body

a stethoscope

6

8 Which piece of medical equipment does a doctor use to listen to your heart?

the speed your heart beats while you are resting - not doing physical activity

walking fast - this is the only healthy activity

tobacco & alcohol

Name the two most common harmful drugs

7

© Chris Jones 2008

VEGETABLE

4 What is 'resting pulse rate'?

3 Which is the odd one out: eating sweets, playing a play station, walking fast or watching TV?

MINERALS

© Chris Jones 2008

Unit 5A

Keeping Healthy

Chatterbox 3   Level 4

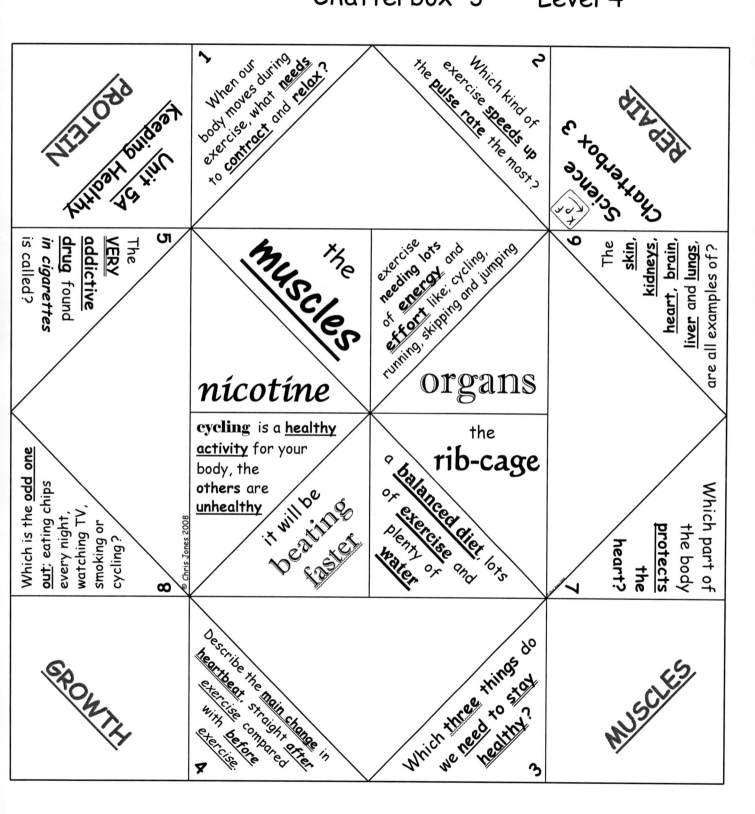

PROTEIN

Keeping Healthy

Unit 5A

REPAIR

Science Chatterbox 3

1 When our body moves during exercise, what **needs** to **contract** and **relax**?

2 Which kind of exercise **speeds up** the **pulse rate** the most?

5 The **VERY addictive drug** found **in cigarettes** is called?

the **muscles**

exercise needing lots of **energy** and **effort** like; cycling, running, skipping and jumping

6 The **skin**, **kidneys**, **heart**, **brain**, **liver** and **lungs**, are all examples of?

nicotine

organs

cycling is a **healthy activity** for your body, the **others** are **unhealthy**

the **rib-cage**

© Chris Jones 2008

it will be beating faster

a **balanced diet**, lots of **exercise** and plenty of **water**

Which part of the body **protects** the **heart**?

Which is the **odd one out**; eating chips every night, watching TV, smoking or cycling?

8

GROWTH

4 Describe the **main change** in **heartbeat**; straight **after exercise** compared with **before exercise**.

3 Which **three things** do we **need** to **stay healthy**?

7

MUSCLES

© Chris Jones 2008

Unit 5A

Keeping Healthy

Chatterbox 4   Level 4

FIBRE

Keeping Healthy

Unit 5A

1 Name just a few ways smoking can <u>damage</u> your lungs

2 Describe some of the main <u>changes</u> to your body when you <u>exercise</u>

Science Chatterbox 4

DIGESTION

5 A person <u>addicted</u> to <u>alcohol</u> is known as ....?

you can get, an awful cough, bronchitis lung cancer, emphysema, breathing problems - as well as covering them with tar.

the <u>heart</u> <u>rate increases</u>, <u>breathing increases</u>, you <u>get hot</u> and <u>sweat more</u>,

in the chest - behind the lungs - and protected by the rib-cage

6 <u>Where</u> <u>about</u> in the body is the <u>heart</u>?

an **alcoholic**

your *lungs*

addicted

it's a **muscle** - when it <u>contracts</u>, it *pumps blood around* the body

<u>Brush your teeth</u>, <u>floss</u> <u>them</u>, and use an <u>anti-plaque</u> <u>mouthwash</u>

How does the heart work?

8 Which <u>organ</u> gets <u>filthy dirty</u> and <u>badly stained</u> <u>with oil</u> when you smoke?

© Chris Jones 2008

ROUGHAGE

4 When someone <u>cannot stop</u> <u>taking harmful drugs</u> e.g. cocaine, heroin, etc they are said to be?

3 What <u>physical action</u> can you take to <u>stop plaque</u> building up between visits to the dentist?

HEALTH

© Chris Jones 2008

Unit 5A

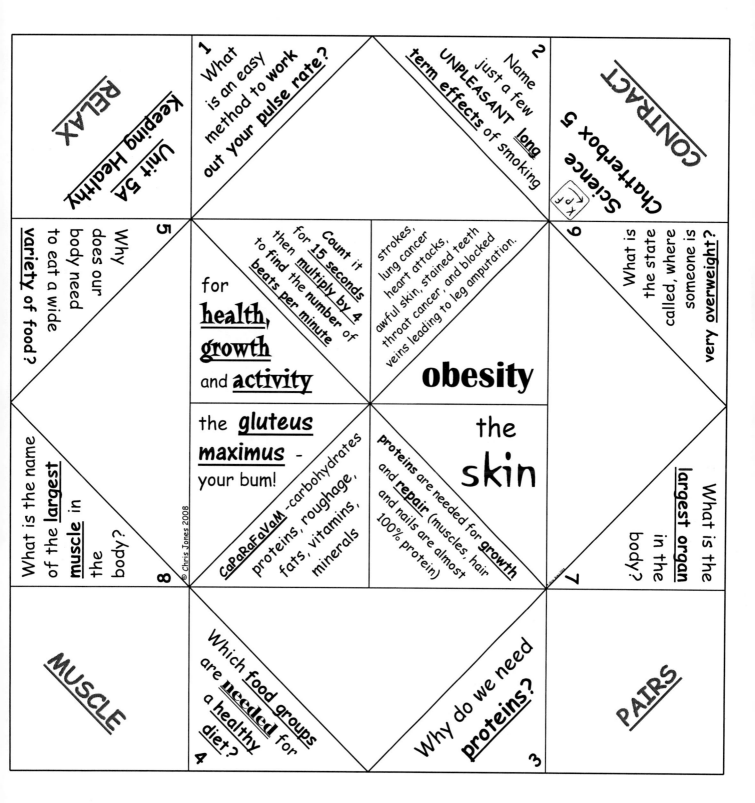

RELAX

Keeping Healthy

Unit 5A

1 What is an easy method to work out your pulse rate?

2 Name just a few UNPLEASANT long term effects of smoking

CONTRACT

Science Chatterbox 5

6 What is the state called, where someone is very overweight?

5 Why does our body need to eat a wide variety of food?

for **health**, **growth** and **activity**

Count it for **15 seconds** then **multiply by 4** to find the number of **beats per minute**

strokes, lung cancer heart attacks, awful skin, stained teeth throat cancer, and blocked veins leading to leg amputation.

obesity

What is the name of the **largest muscle** in the body?

the **gluteus maximus** - your bum!

CaPaRaFaVaM - carbohydrates proteins, roughage, fats, vitamins, minerals

© Chris Jones 2008

Proteins are needed for **growth** and **repair** (muscles, hair and nails are almost 100% protein)

the **skin**

What is the **largest organ** in the body?

MUSCLE

4 Which **food groups** are **needed** for a **healthy diet**?

Why do we need **proteins**?

3

PAIRS

© Chris Jones 2008

Unit 5A

Keeping Healthy

Chatterbox 6   Level 5

EXERCISE

Keeping Healthy

Unit 5A

1 What is the name of the **blood vessel** carrying blood **away from** the heart?

2 Which **activity** results in a **faster pulse**: cycling uphill or walking?

Science Chatterbox 6

SWEATING

5 What do we call the **system** made up of the heart, veins, arteries and capillaries?

an **artery**

the circulatory system

cycling uphill - the muscles **need to work harder**, and use **more energy and oxygen**

the **lungs**

6 Which organ **removes carbon dioxide** from the blood?

veins

oxygen

the muscles **need more oxygen** which is obtained from the lungs

because they need more **oxygen and sugar** - which are carried in the blood

What is the name of the **gas** found in **air** that we **NEED** to **breath**?

7

© Chris Jones 2008

8 What is the name of the **blood vessels** which carry blood **to the** heart?

BREATHING

4 When exercising, we breath **faster** and **deeper**. **Why** is this?

Why do the **muscles need more blood** during exercise?

3

INCREASES

© Chris Jones 2008

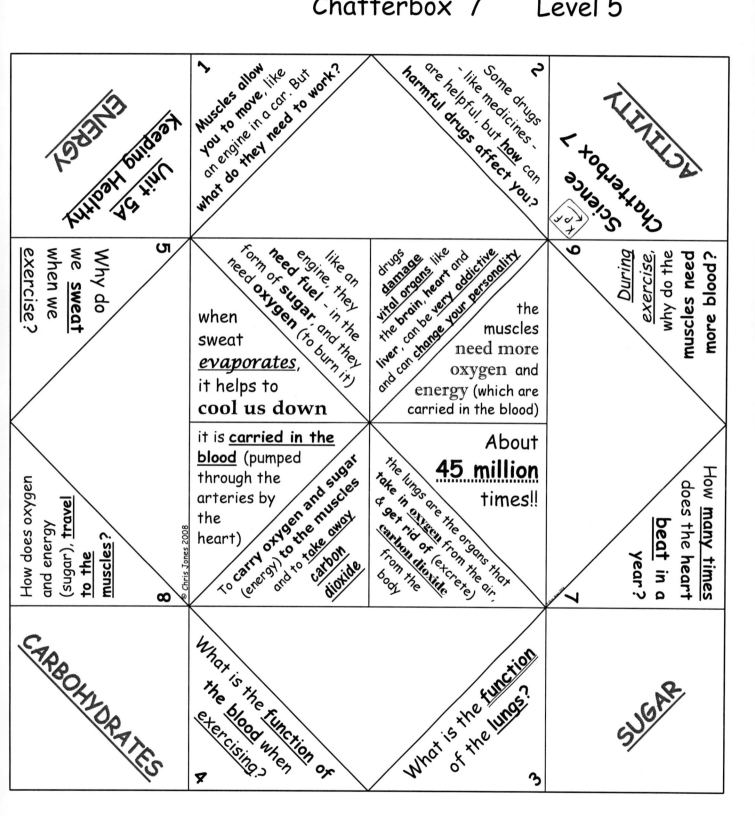

ENERGY

Keeping Healthy Unit 5A

1 Muscles allow you to move, like an engine in a car. But what do they need to work?

2 Some drugs - like medicines - are helpful, but how can harmful drugs affect you?

Science Chatterbox 7

ACTIVITY

5 Why do we sweat when we exercise?

like an engine, they need fuel - in the form of sugar, and they need oxygen (to burn it)

drugs damage vital organs like the brain, heart and liver, can be very addictive and can change your personality

the muscles need more oxygen and energy (which are carried in the blood)

6 During exercise, why do the muscles need more blood?

when sweat evaporates, it helps to cool us down

it is carried in the blood (pumped through the arteries by the heart)

To carry oxygen and sugar (energy) to the muscles and to take away carbon dioxide

the lungs are the organs that take in oxygen from the air, & get rid of (excrete) carbon dioxide from the body

About 45 million times!!

How many times does the heart beat in a year?

How does oxygen and energy (sugar), travel to the muscles?

8 © Chris Jones 2008

CARBOHYDRATES

What is the function of the blood when exercising?

4

What is the function of the lungs?

3

SUGAR

© Chris Jones 2008

Unit 5A

Keeping Healthy

Chatterbox 8   Level 5

ADDICTED

Keeping Healthy

Unit 5A

1 **average** resting pulse is **around 75**. Top athletes have a **resting** pulse rate of **about 50** - what does this tell you about their hearts?

2 Brandon exercises hard -his **pulse rate speeds up**. Then he stops. What happens in the **next 15 minutes**?

Science Chatterbox 8

DRUGS

5 The **system** in our bodies that **turns food** into **energy** is the?

their hearts are **much bigger and stronger** than average -they can pump a much larger amount of blood, with each beat

digestive system

his pulse rate will *steadily decrease* until it finally returns to **resting pulse rate**

her muscles are **working harder**, need **more oxygen and energy** -so the heart needs to **beat faster**

6 Ellie begins to exercise and her **pulse rate increases**. Why does this happen?

about **9 pints!** just over 5 litres

© Chris Jones 2008

muscles also **need oxygen** and **fuel** (sugar) - then **heat**, **movement and CO₂ are produced**

the *respiratory system*

the heart **pumps blood to the lungs** - which then returns back to the heart (now full of O₂)

The nose, mouth, lungs and windpipe form the **system** we **need** for **breathing**, we call this?

7

8 How much blood does the average adult have?

ALCOHOL

4 An engine needs oxygen and fuel (petrol)-then heat, movement and CO₂ are produced. **How are muscles similar?**

There are **2 blood circulation systems** 1ˢᵗ - the heart pumps blood to brain and body - then back to the heart. **What is the second?**

3

TOBACCO

16

© Chris Jones 2008

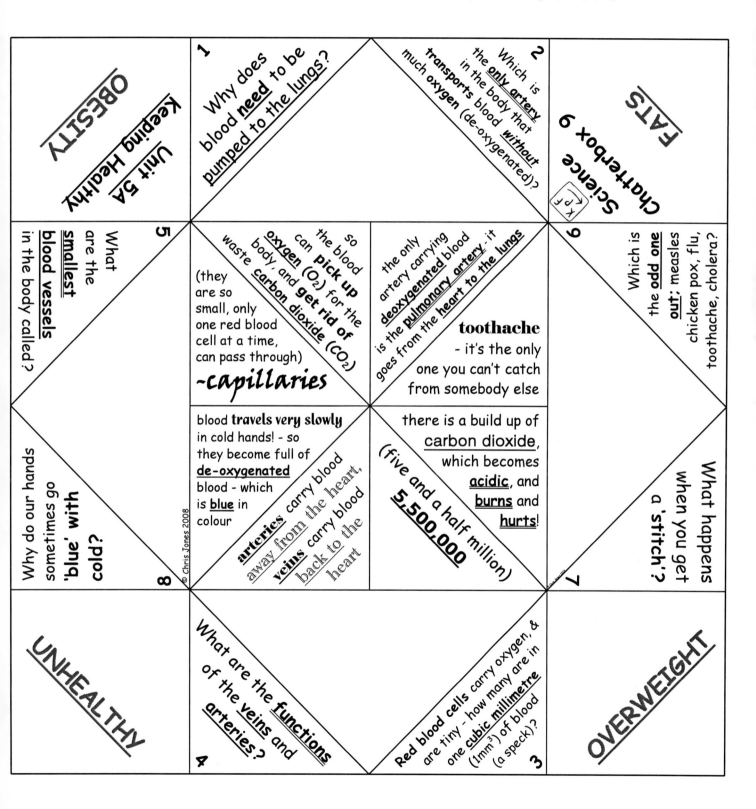

OBESITY

Keeping Healthy

Unit 5A

1 Why does blood **need** to be **pumped to the lungs?**

2 Which is the **only artery** in the body that transports blood **without** much oxygen (de-oxygenated)?

Science Chatterbox 9

FATS

5 What are the **smallest blood vessels** in the body called?

so the blood can **pick up oxygen** (O_2) for the body, and **get rid of** waste **carbon dioxide** (CO_2)

(they are so small, only one red blood cell at a time, can pass through) **~capillaries**

the only artery carrying **deoxygenated** blood - it is the **pulmonary artery** - it goes from the **heart to the lungs**

toothache - it's the only one you can't catch from somebody else

6 Which is the **odd one out**; measles chicken pox, flu, toothache, cholera?

Why do our hands sometimes go **'blue'** with cold?

© Chris Jones 2008

blood **travels very slowly** in cold hands! - so they become full of **de-oxygenated** blood - which is **blue** in colour

arteries carry blood **away from the heart**, **veins** carry blood **back to the heart**

(five and a half million) **5,500,000**

there is a build up of **carbon dioxide**, which becomes **acidic**, and **burns** and **hurts!**

What happens when you get a 'stitch'?

7

8

UNHEALTHY

4 What are the **functions** of the **veins and arteries?**

Red blood cells carry oxygen, & are tiny - how many are in one **cubic millimetre** ($1mm^3$) of blood (a speck)?

3

OVERWEIGHT

© Chris Jones 2008

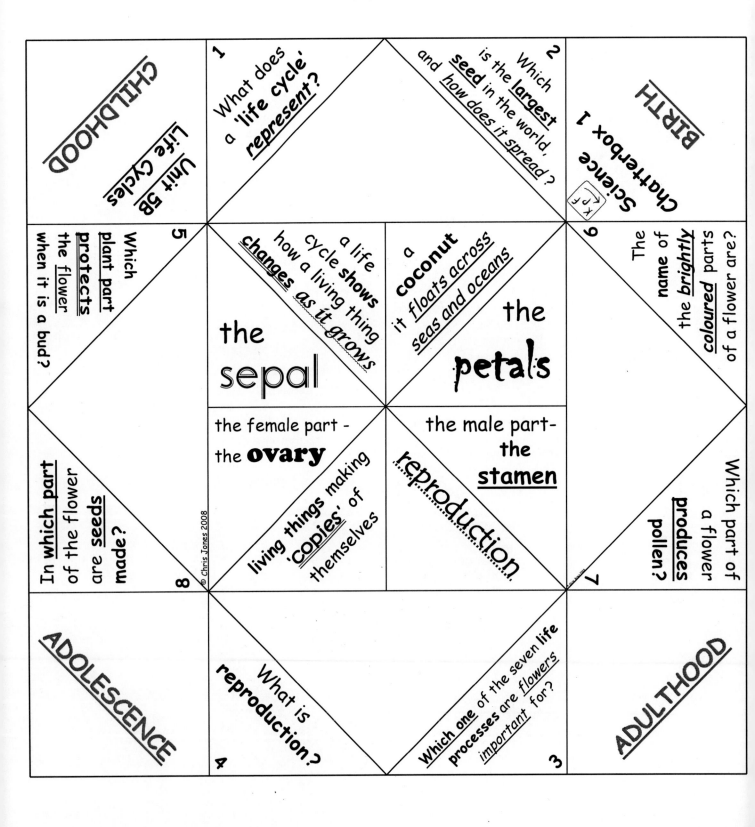

CHILDHOOD

Unit 5B Life Cycles

1 What does a 'life cycle' represent?

2 Which is the largest seed in the world, and how does it spread?

BIRTH

Science Chatterbox 1

5 Which plant part protects the flower when it is a bud?

a life cycle shows how a living thing changes as it grows

a coconut it floats across seas and oceans

the sepal

the petals

6 The name of the brightly coloured parts of a flower are?

In which part of the flower are seeds made?

the female part - the ovary

living things making 'copies' of themselves

the male part - the stamen

reproduction

Which part of a flower produces pollen?

ADOLESCENCE

What is reproduction?

Which one of the seven life processes are flowers important for?

ADULTHOOD

4

3

7

8

© Chris Jones 2008

© Chris Jones 2008

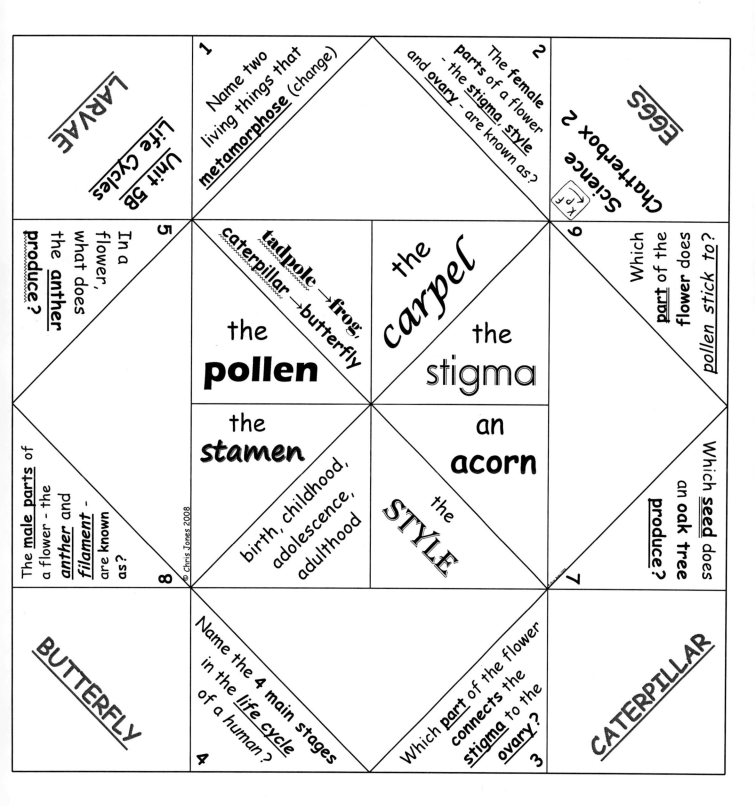

1 Name two living things that metamorphose (change)

2 The female parts of a flower - the stigma, style and ovary - are known as?

Unit 5B Life Cycles

LARVAE

Science Chatterbox 2

EGGS

5 In a flower, what does the anther produce?

tadpole → frog, caterpillar → butterfly

the carpel

6 Which part of the flower does pollen stick to?

the pollen

the stigma

the stamen

birth, childhood, adolescence, adulthood

an acorn

The male parts of a flower - the anther and filament - are known as?

© Chris Jones 2008

the STYLE

Which seed does an oak tree produce?

BUTTERFLY

8

4 Name the 4 main stages in the life cycle of a human?

7

Which part of the flower connects the stigma to the ovary?

3

CATERPILLAR

© Chris Jones 2008

Unit 5B

Life Cycles

Chatterbox 3   Level 4

DISPERSAL

Unit 5B
Life Cycles

1 What are the conditions <u>needed</u> for a <u>seed to germinate</u>?

2 The joining together of a <u>male sex cell</u> (pollen) and a <u>female sex cell</u> (ova) is called?

SEED

Science Chatterbox 3

6 What do we call the <u>process</u> when a <u>seed starts to grow</u>?

5 What is the <u>name</u> of the <u>female sex cells</u> of a plant?

WOW

- <u>warmth</u>, <u>oxygen</u> and <u>water</u>

the **ova** (eggs)

the **ovary**

photosynthesis

fertilisation

germination

the <u>male sex cells</u> of the plant

pollination

© Chris Jones 2008

8 Which <u>part</u> of the flower <u>produces</u> the <u>female sex cells</u>?

What is <u>pollen</u>?

7

WIND

EXCRETION

4 What is the <u>name</u> of the <u>process</u> where <u>plants</u> make food using <u>sunlight</u>?

3 What is the <u>name of the process</u> where <u>pollen</u> travels to the <u>stigma</u>?

© Chris Jones 2008

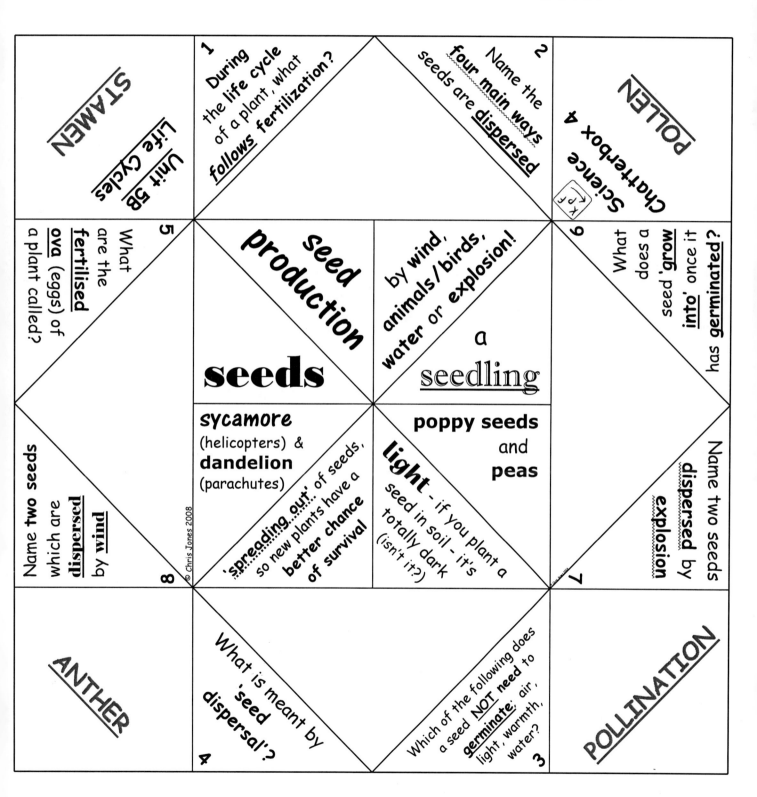

STAMEN

Unit 5B
Life Cycles

POLLEN

Science Chatterbox 4

1 During the life cycle of a plant, what _follows_ fertilization?

2 Name the _four main ways_ seeds are _dispersed_

by wind, animals/birds, water or explosion!

What does a seed _grow into_ once it has _germinated_? **6**

5 What are the _fertilised ova_ (eggs) of a plant called?

seed production

seeds

a **seedling**

sycamore (helicopters) & **dandelion** (parachutes)

poppy seeds and **peas**

'spreading out' of seeds, so new plants have a **better chance of survival**

light - if you plant a seed in soil - it's totally dark (isn't it?)

dispersed by _explosion_

Name two seeds _dispersed_ by _wind_

Name two seeds **7**

© Chris Jones 2008

ANTHER

What is meant by 'seed dispersal'? **4**

Which of the following does a seed _NOT need_ to _germinate_: air, light, warmth, water? **3**

POLLINATION

Life Cycles

Chatterbox 5   Level 4

1 The **female parts** of a plant are?

2 A squirrel buries an acorn then forgets about it - **which part** of the oak tree's **life cycle** is **helped**?

STYLE

Unit 5B Life Cycles

Science Chatterbox 5

STIGMA

5 The **energy needed** for **photosynthesis** comes from?

the **stigma**, **style** and **ovary** (together known as the **carpel**)

SEED DISPERSAL

in summer there is plenty of air and warmth. So - the seed probably **failed to germinate** due to a **lack of water**

6 A seed planted during the summer, had **not germinated** after 4 weeks. What may have been the reason?

sunlight

seed dispersal

the **anther** and **filament** - together known as the **stamen**

insects or **wind**

it could **eat** a fruit such as a berry, then **excrete** the seed many miles away

The **two main ways** that plants are **pollinated** are by?

8 What is the name of the **process** where **seeds spread out - away** from the **plant**?

© Chris Jones 2008

4 Name the **male parts** of a plant

Explain how a **bird** could be important in the process of **seed dispersal**
3

CARPEL

OVARY

© Chris Jones 2008

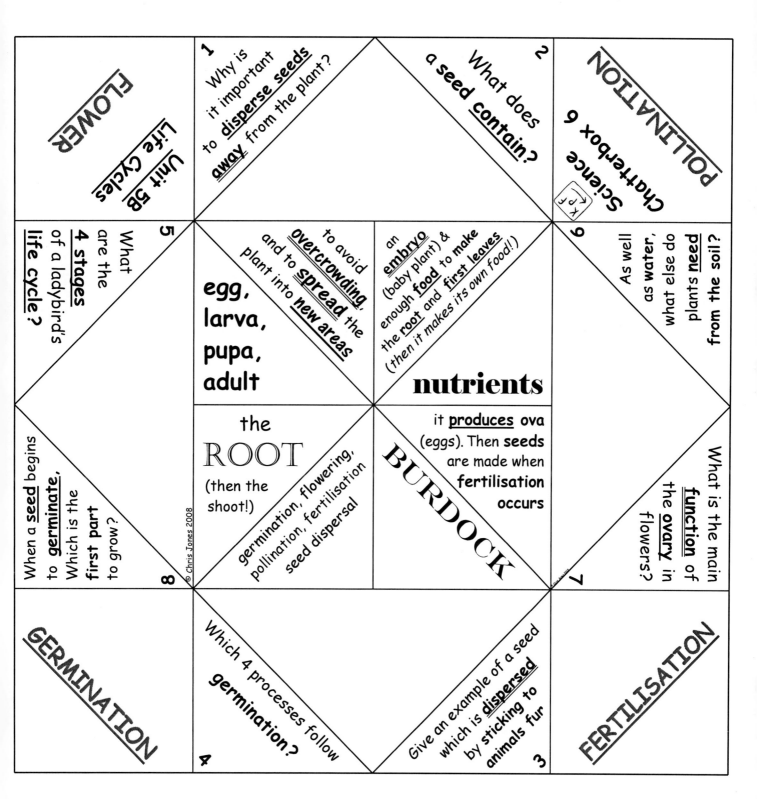

FLOWER

Unit 5B Life Cycles

1 Why is it important to **disperse seeds** **away** from the plant?

2 What does **a seed contain?**

POLLINATION

Science Chatterbox 6

6 As well as water, what else do plants **need** from the soil?

5 What are the **4 stages** of a ladybird's **life cycle?**

to avoid **overcrowding,** and to **spread** the plant into **new areas**

an **embryo** (baby plant) & enough **food** to make the **root** and **first leaves** (*then it makes its own food!*)

egg, larva, pupa, adult

nutrients

the ROOT (then the shoot!)

germination, flowering, pollination, fertilisation seed dispersal

it **produces** ova (eggs). Then **seeds** are made when **fertilisation** occurs

BURDOCK

What is the main **function** of the **ovary** in flowers?

When a **seed** begins to **germinate,** Which is the **first part** to grow?

8

© Chris Jones 2008

GERMINATION

Which 4 processes follow **germination?**

4

Give an example of a seed which is **dispersed** by sticking to animals fur

3

FERTILISATION

7

© Chris Jones 2008

Unit 5B

Life Cycles

Chatterbox 7   Level 5

PHOTOSYNTHESIS

Life Cycles

Unit 5B

1 Why do frogs and tadpoles live in **different habitats** and have **different diets**?

2 What is the **chemical formula** for **photosynthesis**?

CHLOROPHYLL

Science Chatterbox 7

6 What is the name of the **green pigment** found in leaves?

5 What is the **chemical formula** for **sugar**?

so they **don't compete with each other** for space and food

$$6H_2O + 6CO_2 \xrightarrow{\text{sunlight}} C_6H_{12}O_6 + 6O_2$$

$C_6H_{12}O_6$

if a plant or animal **didn't reproduce**, then it would **become** EXTINCT

© Chris Jones 2008

it is needed for pollination

H_2O and CO_2

the plant takes in **carbon dioxide** and **water** → making **sugar** & releasing **oxygen** back into the **air**

chlorophyll

Reproduction is very important for living things. **Why**?

Why is a bee so **important** in the **life cycle** of flowering plants?

8

7

METAMORPHOSIS

4 What is the **chemical formulae** for **water** and **carbon dioxide**?

3 What happens during **photosynthesis**?

REPRODUCTION

© Chris Jones 2008

SOLID

Gases Around Us

Unit 5C

1

What is
air made of?

2

What is
the **process**
where a solid
changes into a liquid?

Science
Chatterbox 1

GAS

5

What
do we call
'<u>friction</u>
<u>in air</u>'?

a mixture
of <u>gases</u>, such as
nitrogen, oxygen
and **carbon dioxide**

air
resistance

melting

gas
solid
and **liquid**

6

What
are the
three states
of matter?

OXYGEN

freezing

condensation

evaporation

This **gas** is in
the air – we
use it to
breath

© Chris Jones 2008

8

Name the **process**
where a liquid
changes
<u>into</u> a
solid ?

7

LIQUID

What is the **process**
where a **gas**
changes into
liquid?

4

Name the **process** where
a liquid changes
<u>into</u> a gas

3

STATE

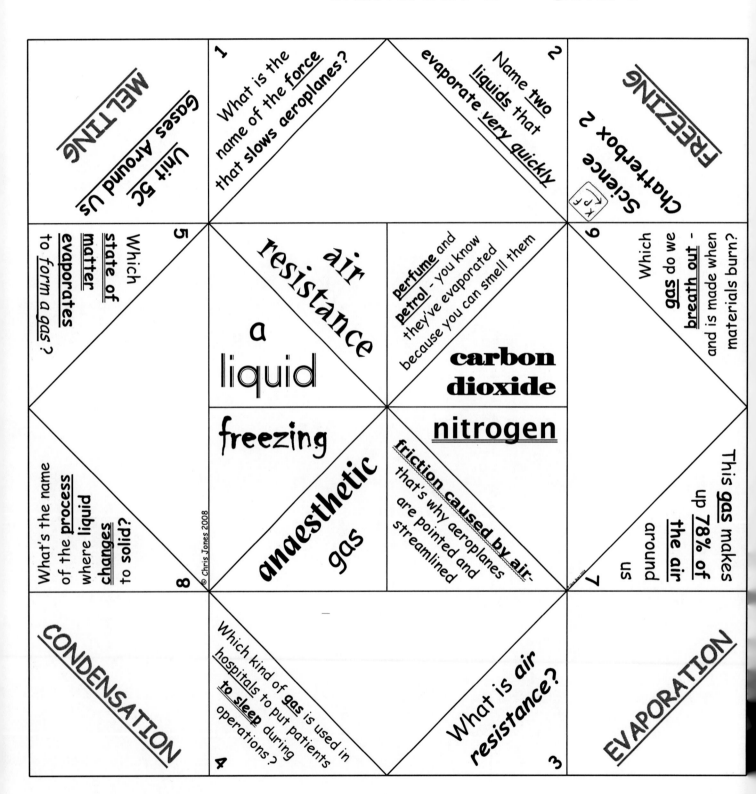

MELTING

Gases Around Us

Unit 5C

1 What is the name of the force that slows aeroplanes?

Name two liquids that evaporate very quickly **2**

FREEZING

Science Chatterbox 2

5 Which state of matter evaporates to form a gas?

air resistance

a liquid

perfume and petrol - you know they've evaporated because you can smell them

carbon dioxide

nitrogen

Which gas do we breath out - and is made when materials burn? **6**

freezing

anaesthetic gas

friction caused by air - that's why aeroplanes are pointed and streamlined

This gas makes up 78% of the air around us

© Chris Jones 2008

What's the name of the process where liquid changes to solid? **8**

Which kind of gas is used in hospitals to put patients to sleep during operations? **4**

What is air resistance? **3**

CONDENSATION

EVAPORATION

© Chris Jones 2008

Unit 5C

Gases Around Us

Chatterbox 3   Level 3

OXYGEN

Gases Around Us

Unit 5C

1 What happens when a material **condensates**?

2 This **gas** is found in airships and helps them to **float**

Science Chatterbox 1

NITROGEN

5 What happens when a material **melts**?

it **changes** from the **gas state** to the **liquid state**

it **changes** from the **solid state** to the **liquid state**

helium

gas bubbles (usually CO_2)

6

In 'fizzy' drinks, what is the 'fizz'?

Which **unit of measure** is used to measure **volumes of liquids**?

MILLILITRES & LITRES

it **changes** from the **liquid state** to the solid state

carbon dioxide (CO_2)

they **change** from the **liquid state** into the **gas state**

What happens when materials **evaporate**?

8

© Chris Jones 2008

7

AIR

4 What happens when a material **freezes**?

Which **gas** is used in some fire extinguishers?

3

CARBON DIOXIDE

Unit 5C

Gases Around Us

Chatterbox 4　　　Level 3

HELIUM

Gases Around Us

Unit 5C

1 When talking about global warming, what is _carbon dioxide called_?

2 What's the name of the **process** where a liquid **changes** to gas?

Science Chatterbox 4

HYDROGEN

5 Where does the **gas** used in **gas cookers** in the home, come from?

the green house gas

from deep in the ground under the **North Sea**

EVAPORATION

melting

6 What do we call the **process** where a solid **changes** to liquid?

nitrous oxide

condensation

oxygen

because there is _more_ _air resistance,_ a force which _slows you_ _down_

Which gas do we **need** to **breath?**

What is the proper name for the gas we call _laughing_ _gas?_

8

© Chris Jones 2008

4 What's the name of the **process** where gas **changes to** a liquid?

Why does walking into the wind on a windy day _need more_ _energy?_

3

7

METHANE

COMPRESS

28

© Chris Jones 2008

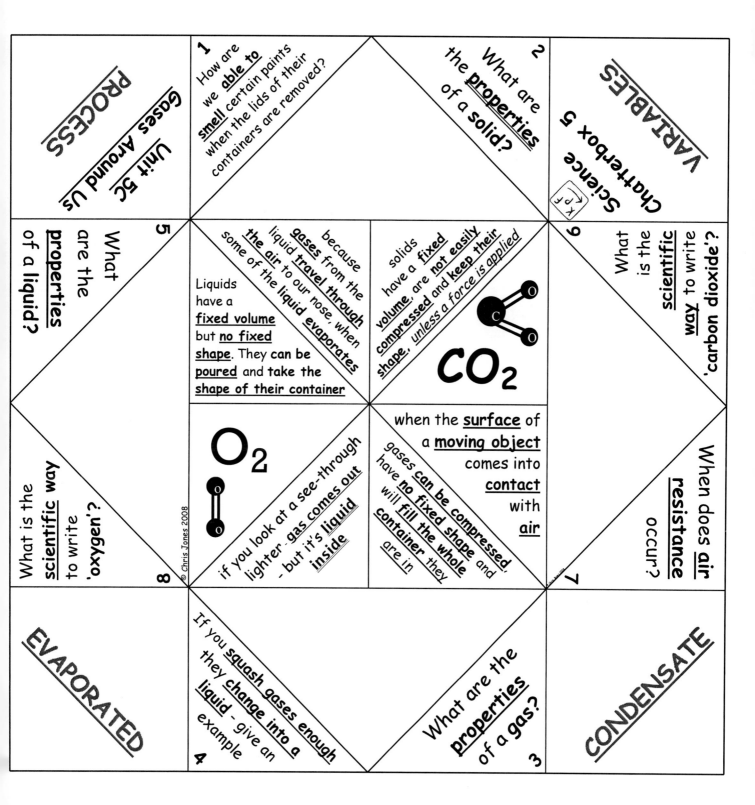

PROCESS

Gases Around Us

Unit 5C

1 How are we **able to** **smell** certain paints when the lids of their containers are removed?

2 What are the **properties** of a **solid**?

VARIABLES

Science Chatterbox 5

because **gases** from the liquid **travel through** **the air** to our nose, when some of the liquid **evaporates**

solids have a **fixed** **volume**, are **not easily** **compressed** and **keep their** **shape**, *unless a force is applied*

CO_2

6 What is the **scientific** **way** to write 'carbon dioxide'?

5 What are the **properties** of a **liquid**?

Liquids have a **fixed volume** but **no fixed** **shape**. They **can be** **poured** and take the **shape of their container**

O_2

© Chris Jones 2008

if you look at a see-through lighter, gas comes out - but it's **liquid** **inside**

when the **surface** of a **moving object** comes into **contact** with **air**

gases can be compressed, have **no fixed shape** and will **fill the whole** **container** they are in

When does **air** **resistance** occur?

What is the **scientific way** to write 'oxygen'?

8

EVAPORATED

If you **squash gases enough** they **change into a** **liquid** - give an example

4

What are the **properties** of a **gas**?

3

CONDENSATE

7

Unit 5C

Gases Around Us

Chatterbox 6   Level 4

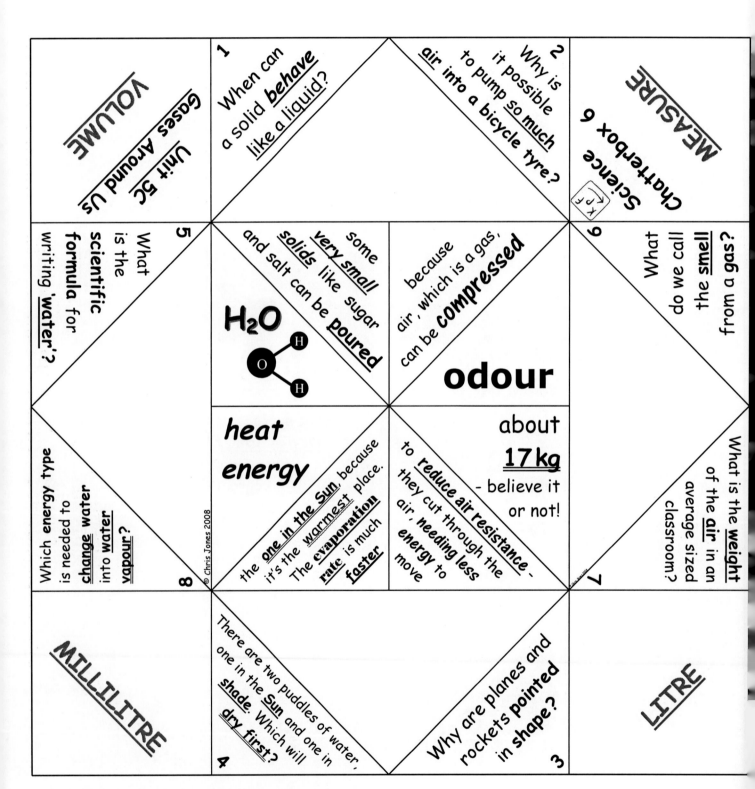

VOLUME

Gases Around Us

Unit 5C

1 When can a solid **behave** like a liquid?

2 Why is it possible to pump so much **air** into a bicycle tyre?

MEASURE

Science Chatterbox 6

What do we call the **smell** from a gas?

5 What is the scientific **formula** for writing '**water**'?

some **very small** **solids** like sugar and salt can be **poured**

H_2O

H O H

because air, which is a gas, can be **compressed**

odour

What is the **weight** of the **air** in an average sized classroom?

Which energy type is needed to **change** water into water **vapour**?

heat energy

the **one in the Sun**, because it's the **warmest** place. The **evaporation** **rate** is much **faster**

© Chris Jones 2008

to **reduce air resistance** - they cut through the air, needing less energy to move

about **17 kg** - believe it or not!

8

7

MILLILITRE

There are two puddles of water, one in the **Sun** and one in **shade**. Which will **dry first**?

Why are planes and rockets **pointed** in **shape**?

LITRE

4

3

© Chris Jones 2008

Unit 5C

Gases Around Us

Chatterbox 7   Level 5

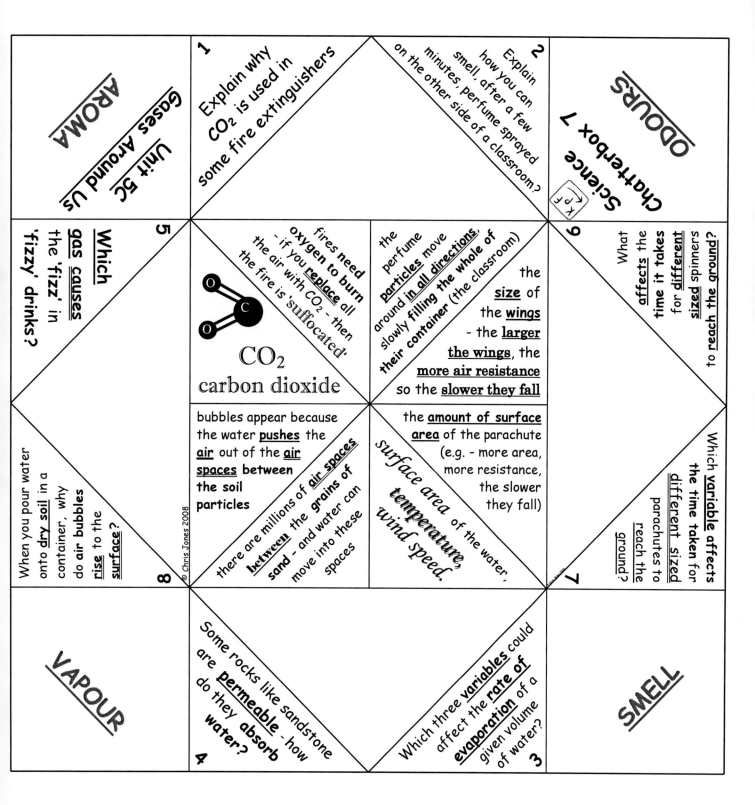

AROMA

Gases Around Us

Unit 5C

1 Explain why CO_2 is used in some fire extinguishers

2 Explain how you can smell, after a few minutes, perfume sprayed on the other side of a classroom?

Science
Chatterbox 7

ODOURS

5 Which gas causes the 'fizz' in 'fizzy' drinks?

fires need oxygen to burn - if you replace all the air with CO_2 - then the fire is 'suffocated'

the perfume particles move around in all directions, slowly filling the whole of their container (the classroom)

the size of the wings - the larger the wings, the more air resistance so the slower they fall

6 What affects the time it takes for different sized spinners to reach the ground?

CO_2 carbon dioxide

bubbles appear because the water pushes the air out of the air spaces between the soil particles

there are millions of air spaces between the grains of sand - and water can move into these spaces

the amount of surface area of the parachute (e.g. - more area, more resistance, the slower they fall)

surface area of the water, temperature, wind speed.

Which variable affects the time taken for different sized parachutes to reach the ground?

© Chris Jones 2008

When you pour water onto dry soil in a container, why do air bubbles rise to the surface?

8

VAPOUR

Some rocks like sandstone are permeable - how do they absorb water?

4

Which three variables could affect the rate of evaporation of a given volume of water?

3

SMELL

7

© Chris Jones 2008

Unit 5C

Gases Around Us

Chatterbox 8   Level 5

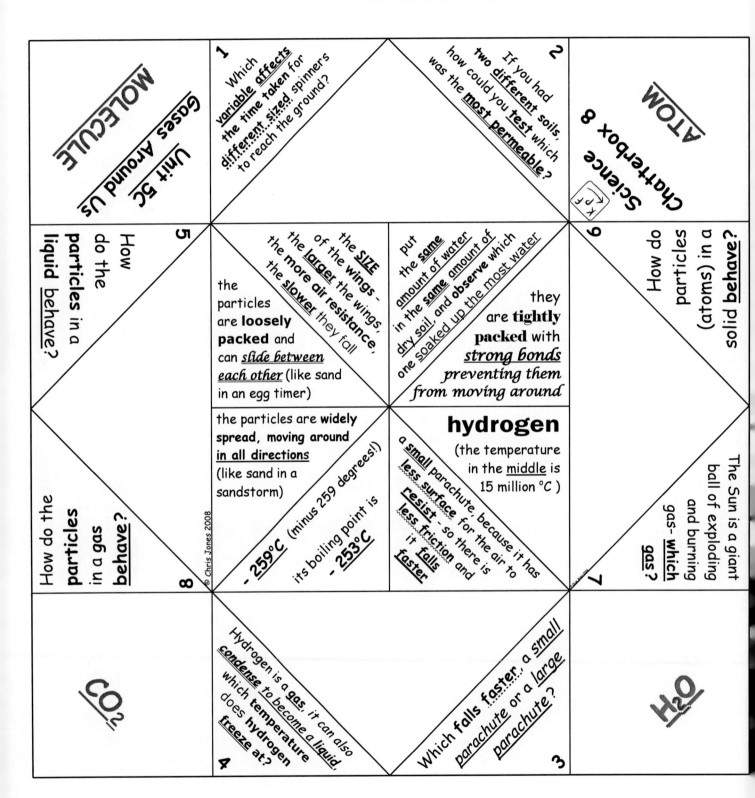

1 Which variable _affects_ the time taken for different sized spinners to reach the ground?

2 If you had two _different_ soils, how could you _test_ which was the _most permeable_?

Unit 5C
Gases Around Us
MOLECULE

Science
Chatterbox 8
ATOM

5 How do the particles in a liquid _behave_?

the _SIZE_ of the wings - the _larger_ the wings, the _more air resistance_, the _slower_ they fall

the particles are **loosely packed** and can _slide between each other_ (like sand in an egg timer)

put the _same_ amount of water in the _same_ amount of dry soil, and _observe_ which one soaked up the most water

they are **tightly packed** with _strong bonds_ preventing them from moving around

6 How do particles (atoms) in a solid _behave_?

How do the particles in a gas _behave_?

the particles are **widely spread, moving around in all directions** (like sand in a sandstorm)

- _259_°C (minus 259 degrees!) its boiling point is - 253°C

hydrogen (the temperature in the _middle_ is 15 million °C)

a _small_ parachute, because it has _less surface_ for the air to _resist_ - so there is _less friction_ and it _falls faster_

The Sun is a giant ball of exploding and burning gas- _which_ gas?

© Chris Jones 2008

8

CO₂

Hydrogen is a gas, it can also _condense_ to become a liquid, which _temperature_ does **hydrogen** _freeze_ at?

4

Which falls _faster_, a _small parachute_ or a _large parachute_?

3

7

H₂O

32

© Chris Jones 2008

Unit 5D

Changing State

Chatterbox 1   Level 3

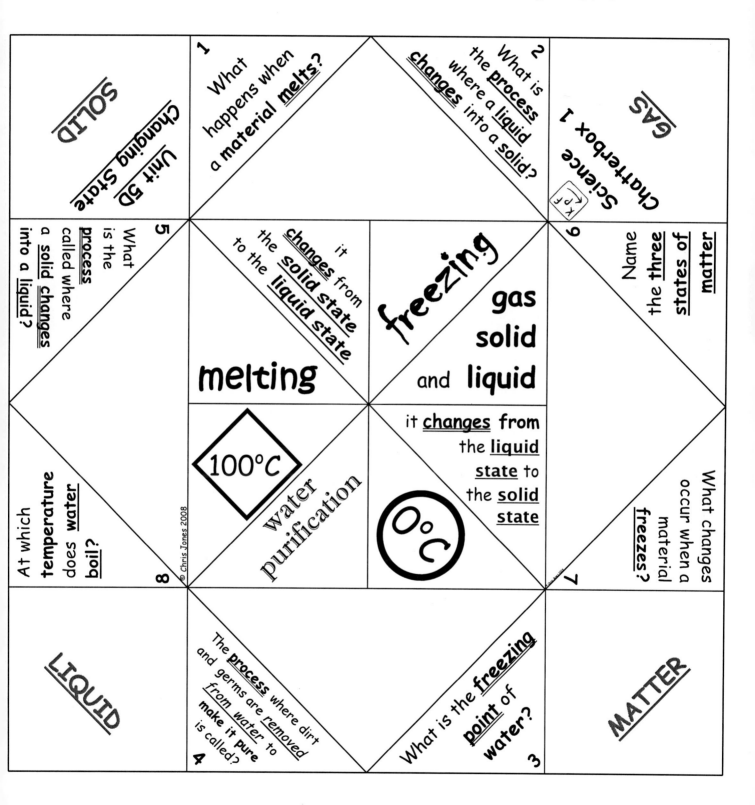

1 - What happens when a material **melts**?

2 - What is the **process** where a **liquid** **changes** into a **solid**?

SOLID

Changing State Unit 5D

Science Chatterbox 1

GAS

5 - What is the **process** called where a **solid changes** into a **liquid**?

it **changes** from the **solid state** to the **liquid state**

freezing

gas solid and liquid

6 - Name the **three states of matter**

melting

100°C

water purification

it **changes** from the **liquid state** to the **solid state**

0°C

What changes occur when a material **freezes**?

At which **temperature** does **water boil**?

8

© Chris Jones 2008

LIQUID

4 - The **process** where dirt and germs are **removed** from **water** to **make it pure** is called?

What is the **freezing point** of **water**?

3

MATTER

7

© Chris Jones 2008

33

Unit 5D

Changing State

Chatterbox 2   Level 3

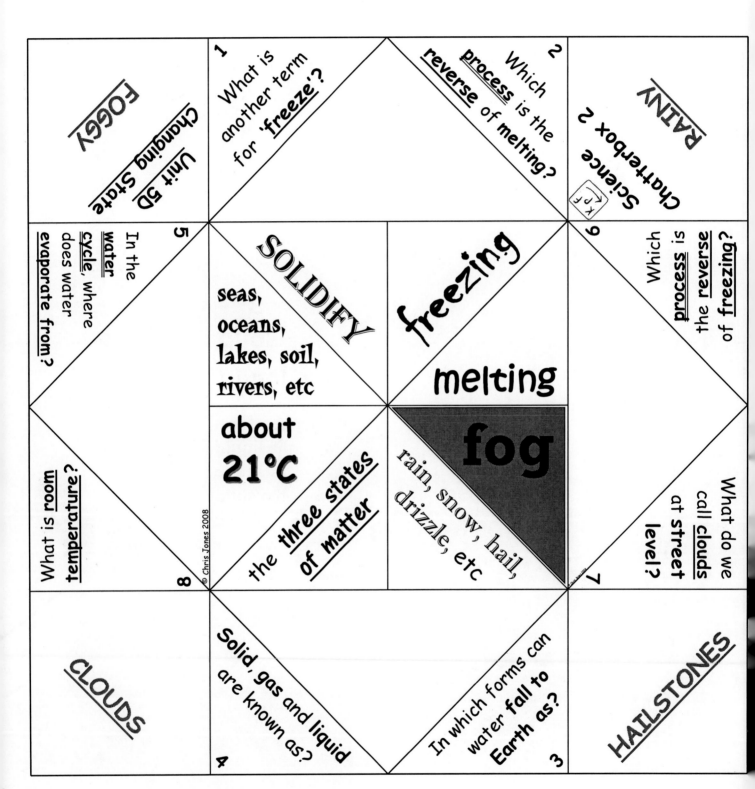

1 — What is another term for 'freeze'?

2 — Which process is the reverse of melting?

FOGGY

Unit 5D Changing State

Science Chatterbox 2 — RAINY

5 — In the water cycle, where does water evaporate from?

SOLIDIFY

seas, oceans, lakes, soil, rivers, etc

freezing

melting

fog

6 — Which process is the reverse of freezing?

What is room temperature?

about 21°C

the three states of matter

rain, snow, hail, drizzle, etc

What do we call clouds at street level?

© Chris Jones 2008

8

7

CLOUDS

Solid, gas and liquid are known as?

In which forms can water fall to Earth as?

HAILSTONES

4

3

© Chris Jones 2008

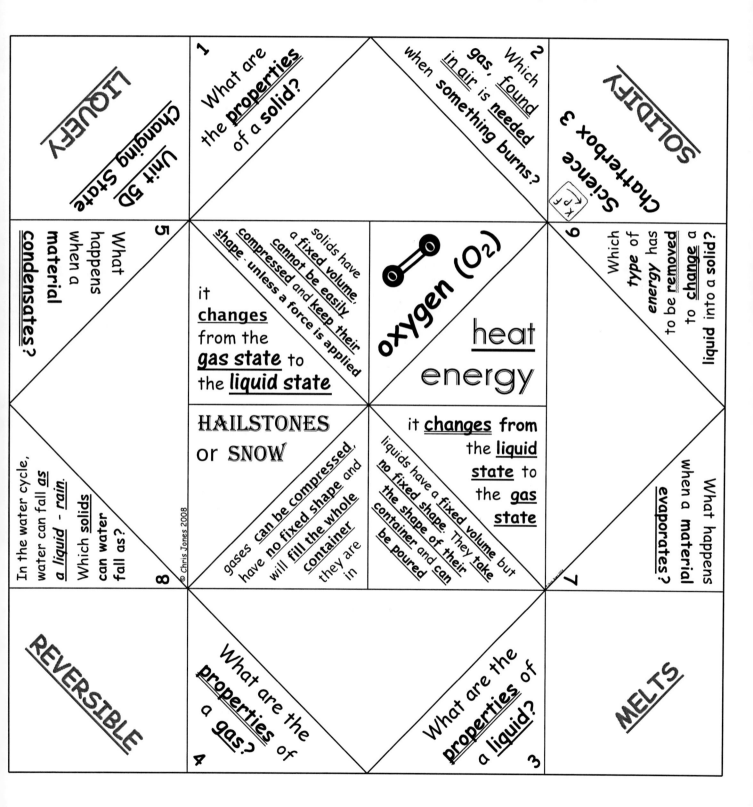

LIQUEFY

Unit 5D Changing State

1 What are the **properties** of a **solid**?

2 Which **gas**, **found** **in air** is **needed** when **something burns**?

Science Chatterbox 3

SOLIDIFY

5 What happens when a material **condensates**?

solids have a **fixed volume**, cannot be easily **compressed** and **keep their shape** - unless a force is applied

it **changes** from the **gas state** to the **liquid state**

oxygen (O₂)

heat energy

6 Which **type of** **energy** has to be **removed** to **change** a **liquid into a solid**?

In the water cycle, water can fall **as a liquid - rain**. Which **solids** can water fall as?

HAILSTONES or SNOW

© Chris Jones 2008

gases **can be compressed**, have **no fixed shape** and will **fill the whole** **container** they are in

liquids have a **fixed volume** but **no fixed shape**. They take **the shape of their** **container** and **can** **be poured**

it **changes** from the **liquid** **state** to the **gas** **state**

7 What happens when a material **evaporates**?

8

REVERSIBLE

4 What are the **properties** of a **gas**?

3 What are the **properties** of a **liquid**?

MELTS

© Chris Jones 2008

Unit 5D

Changing State

Chatterbox 4   Level 4

STATE

Unit 5D Changing State

1 Which two **reversible** **processes** does the Earth **depend on** to get **fresh clean rainwater**?

2 Water is constantly **evaporating** and **condensating** on Earth. What is this **system** known as?

Science Chatterbox 4

CHANGE

5 Some wet towels are on a radiator. Name the **process** that causes them to **dry completely**.

evaporation and **condensation**

EVAPORATION

the water cycle

HEAT ENERGY

6 Which **type of energy** is needed to **change water** into **water vapour**?

carbon dioxide (CO_2)

© Chris Jones 2008

the one in the **Sun**, because it's in the **warmest place**. The **evaporation rate** will be **faster**

condensation

the **volume remains the same**, but it takes on the **shape of the new container**

What is the name of the **process** where a **gas becomes liquid**?

8 Which **gas** is **produced** when something is **burned**?

4 There are two puddles of water, one in **sunlight** and one in **shade**. Which will **dry first**?

What happens when a **liquid is poured into** a **different container**?

3

PROCESS

PROPERTY

© Chris Jones 2008

Unit 5D

Changing State

Chatterbox 5   Level 4

MELTING

Changing State

Unit 5D

1 Briefly explain the <u>processes</u> happening in the <u>water cycle</u>

2 Wet clothes are on a washing line, name the <u>process</u> that causes them to <u>dry completely</u>

FREEZING

Science Chatterbox 5

5 Which <u>states</u> of <u>matter</u> are able to <u>flow</u> through a hose?

water from lakes, rivers and seas <u>evaporates</u> into the air. As it <u>COOLS</u>, it <u>condenses</u> and falls as rain or snow

evaporation

gas or liquid

evaporation

the

sun

GAS

6 What provides the <u>energy</u> for the <u>water cycle</u> to happen?

© Chris Jones 2008

condensation is the <u>reverse</u> of which <u>process?</u>

evaporation –its root word is **vapour** which means – *the gas form of a liquid.* Therefore evaporation means, *'to change from a liquid into a gas'*.

con<u>dens</u>ation. The root word is from the Latin - **densus** (thick). Condense means *'to become thick'.* Therefore, condensation is *'the process of becoming thicker'* (water vapour → water liquid)

7 Which <u>state of matter</u> can be <u>squashed</u> into a <u>smaller volume?</u>

8

EVAPORATION

4 What is a useful way for *remembering* what <u>evaporation</u> means?

3 What is a useful way for *remembering* what <u>condensation</u> means?

CONDENSATION

© Chris Jones 2008

37

Unit 5D

Changing State

Chatterbox 6   Level 4

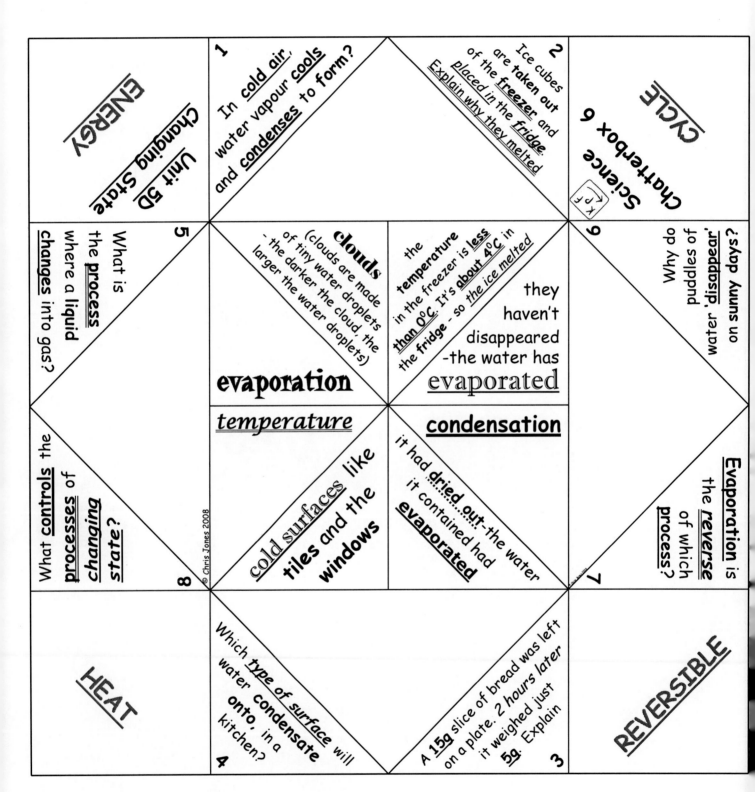

ENERGY

Unit 5D Changing State

1 In **cold air**, water vapour <u>cools</u> and <u>condenses</u> to **form?**

2 Ice cubes are taken out of the **freezer** and placed in the **fridge**. <u>Explain why they melted.</u>

CYCLE

Science Chatterbox 6

Why do puddles of water 'disappear' on sunny days?

5 What is the **process** where a **liquid** <u>changes</u> into gas?

clouds (clouds are made of tiny water droplets - the darker the cloud, the larger the water droplets)

the temperature in the freezer is <u>less</u> than 0°C. It's <u>about 4°C</u> in the fridge - so *the ice melted*

they haven't disappeared -the water has **evaporated**

evaporation

temperature

condensation

What <u>controls</u> the **processes** of *changing* *state?*

© Chris Jones 2008

cold surfaces like tiles and the windows

it had <u>dried out</u>-the water it contained had **evaporated**

Evaporation is the *reverse* of which *process?*

HEAT

4 Which **type of surface** will water **condensate** **onto**, in a kitchen?

3 A <u>15g</u> slice of bread was left on a plate. 2 hours later it weighed just <u>5g</u>. Explain

REVERSIBLE

© Chris Jones 2008

TEMPERATURE

Changing State Unit 5D

1 How do the **particles** in a **liquid behave?**

2 How do we know that air **contains water vapour?**

CHANGING

Science Chatterbox 7

6 What is the **effect** of the outside **temperature** on the **rate** that washing dries?

the particles are **less tightly packed** and can slide between each other (like sand in an egg timer)

because if you expose a **cold surface**, such as a can from the fridge, water **condensates** onto it

the **warmer** it is outside, the **quicker** the washing will **dry**

water vapour in the air will **condensate** onto the **cold surface** of the can

5 A can of coke is taken out of the fridge. It will quickly **become wet on the outside. Explain why**

the **windier** it is, the **FASTER** the washing **dries**

the particles are **widely spread, moving about in all directions** (like sand in a sandstorm)

as a **solid**, particles are joined by bonds between each other. As it heats the particles **vibrate violently** – **breaking these bonds** – and start to move freely. **It's melted**

her breath contains water **vapour which condenses onto the mirror's cold surface**

8 What **effect** does the amount of wind have on the **rate** that washing dries?

© Chris Jones 2008

How do the **particles in a gas behave?** **7**

LIQUEFY

3 Lucy breathes onto a mirror which **becomes misty. Explain why**

4 Explain what happens inside a material when it **melts**

SOLIDIFICATION

© Chris Jones 2008

Unit 5E

Earth, Sun and Moon

Chatterbox 1   Level 3

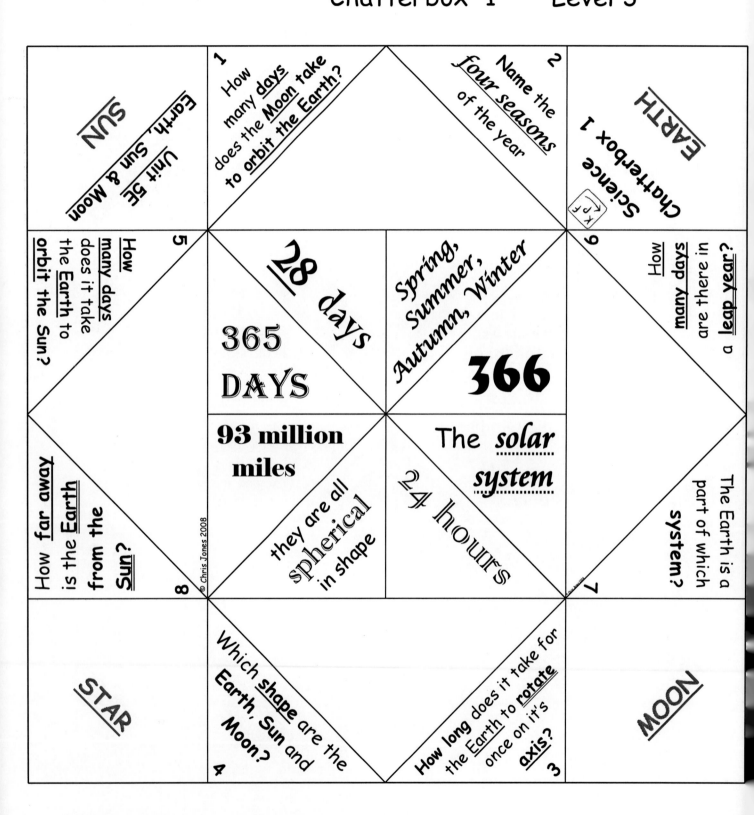

SUN

Earth, Sun & Moon Unit 5E

1 How many days does the Moon take to orbit the Earth?

Name the four seasons of the year 2

Science Chatterbox 1 EARTH

5 How many days does it take the Earth to orbit the Sun?

28 days

365 DAYS

93 million miles

Spring, Summer, Autumn, Winter

366

The solar system

24 hours

How many days are there in a leap year? 6

How far away is the Earth from the Sun?

© Chris Jones 2008

they are all spherical in shape

The Earth is a part of which system? 7

STAR

Which shape are the Earth, Sun and Moon? 4

How long does it take for the Earth to rotate once on it's axis? 3

MOON

© Chris Jones 2008

Unit 5E

Earth, Sun and Moon

Chatterbox 2   Level 3

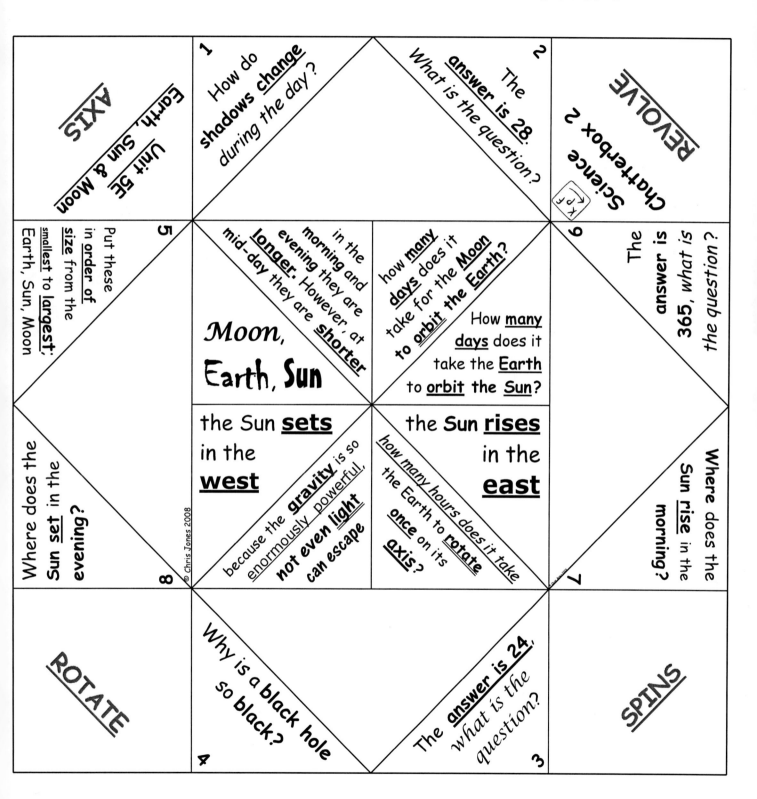

AXIS

Earth, Sun & Moon

Unit 5E

1 How do **shadows change** during the day?

2 The **answer is 28**. What is the question?

Science Chatterbox 2

REVOLVE

The **answer is 365**, what is the question?

5 Put these in **order of size** from the **smallest** to **largest**; Earth, Sun, Moon

in the morning and evening they are **longer**. However, at mid-day they are **shorter**

Moon, Earth, Sun

how **many days** does it take for the **Moon** to **orbit the Earth?**

How **many days** does it take the **Earth** to **orbit** the **Sun?**

Where does the Sun **set** in the **evening?**

the Sun **sets** in the **west**

© Chris Jones 2008

because the **gravity** is so enormously powerful, **not even light** can escape

how many hours does it take the Earth to **rotate** **once** on its **axis?**

the Sun **rises** in the **east**

Where does the Sun **rise** in the morning?

ROTATE

8

Why is a black hole so **black?**

4

The **answer is 24**, what is the question?

3

SPINS

7

6

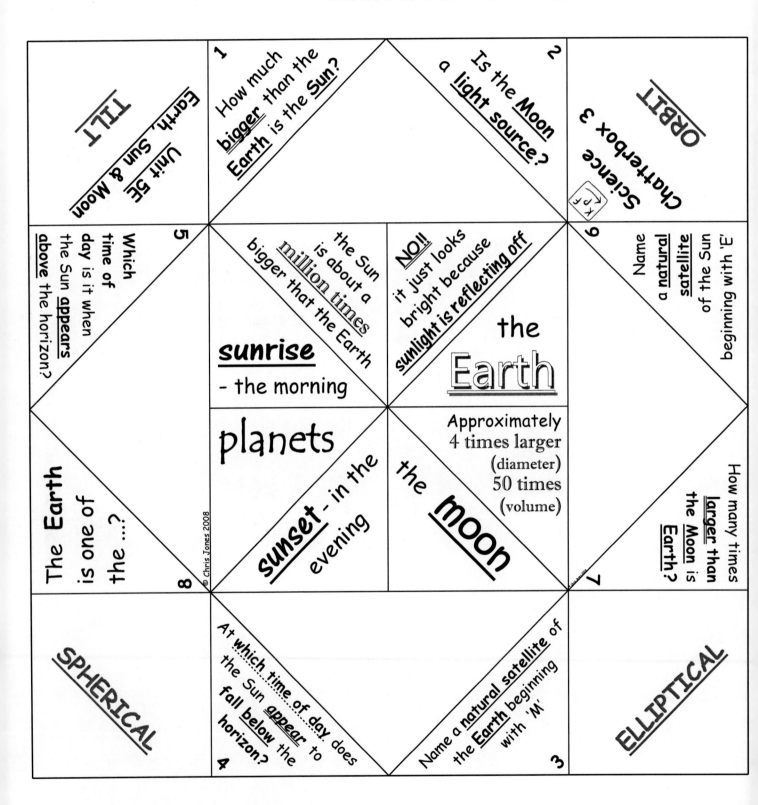

TILT

Earth, Sun & Moon Unit 5E

1 How much **bigger** than the **Earth** is the **Sun**?

2 Is the **Moon** a **light source**?

Science Chatterbox 3

ORBIT

5 Which time of day is it when the Sun **appears** **above** the horizon?

the Sun is about a **million times** bigger that the Earth

sunrise - the morning

NO!! it just looks bright because **sunlight is reflecting off**

6 Name a **natural satellite** of the Sun beginning with 'E'

the **Earth**

The Earth is one of the ...?

planets

sunset - in the evening

the **moon**

Approximately 4 times larger (diameter) 50 times (volume)

How many times **larger than** the Moon is **Earth**?

SPHERICAL

8

© Chris Jones 2008

At **which time of day** does the Sun **appear** to **fall below** the horizon?

4

Name a **natural satellite** of the **Earth** beginning with 'M'

3

7

ELLIPTICAL

42

© Chris Jones 2008

Unit 5E

Earth, Sun and Moon

Chatterbox 4   Level 4

EAST

Earth, Sun & Moon

Unit 5E

1 Which time of the year has the longest daylight hours?

2 Which time of the year has the shortest daylight hours?

Science Chatterbox 4

SUNRISE

5 What time is it on the part of the Earth facing the Sun?

the summer months. June 21st is the longest day - 'midsummer's day'

the winter months. December 21st is the shortest day

6 What is the name for the path that the Earth takes around the Sun?

day time

an ORBIT

astronomy

the Earth rotating on its axis

The study of planets, stars, comets, galaxies and space, is known as what?

NO, it appears to move because the Earth is spinning on its axis

because the Earth is tilted towards the Sun, so its rays are more concentrated

What causes night and day?

© Chris Jones 2008

8

7

SHADOWS

4 Does the Sun actually move across the sky?

3 Why is it warmer in some months of the year?

LONGER

© Chris Jones 2008

43

WEST

Earth, Sun & Moon   Unit 5E

1 What time of day is it on the part of the Earth facing away from the Sun?

2 Why does the Sun appear to move across the sky?

Science Chatterbox 5

SUNSET

In Britain, is daytime in November the same, longer or shorter than July? **5**

Night time because everything is in **darkness**

it's **shorter** - because the Earth is **tilted away from the Sun**

because the Earth is **rotating** (spinning) on it's **axis**

(28)

How many **days** are there in a **lunar month**? **6**

If there is a **full Moon** on **August 1st**. On **which date** will the next one be?

on **August 29th** - 28 days later

in **summer**, the Sun **rises earlier** in the morning & **sets later** in the evening than in **winter**

because it's **held in place** by **gravity** from the Earth

about **25,000 miles (40,000 Km)**

Why doesn't all the **air** in our atmosphere **float into space**? **7**

© Chris Jones 2008 **8**

LUNAR

4 What's the **difference** between **sunrise and sunset times** in **winter** and **summer**?

How far is it from where you are standing, all the way **around the Earth and back again**? **3**

METEORITE

© Chris Jones 2008

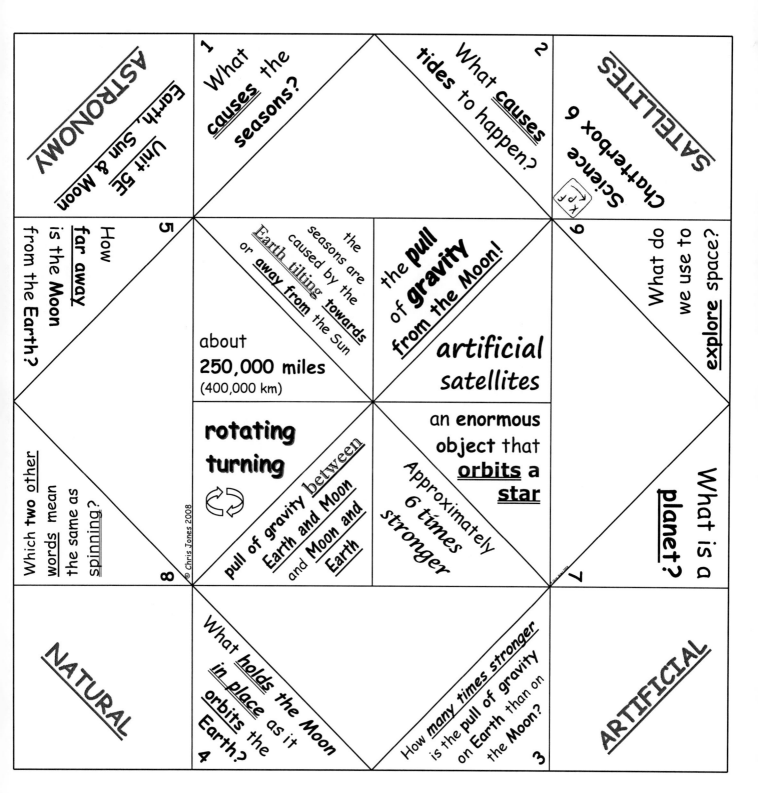

ASTRONOMY

Unit 5E Earth, Sun & Moon

1 What causes the seasons?

2 What causes tides to happen?

SATELLITES

Science Chatterbox 6

5 How far away is the Moon from the Earth?

the seasons are caused by the Earth tilting towards or away from the Sun

the pull of gravity from the Moon!

6 What do we use to explore space?

about 250,000 miles (400,000 km)

artificial satellites

rotating turning

© Chris Jones 2008

pull of gravity between Earth and Moon and Moon and Earth

an enormous object that orbits a star

Approximately 6 times stronger

Which two other words mean the same as spinning?

8

What is a planet?

7

NATURAL

What holds the Moon in place as it orbits the Earth?

4

How many times stronger is the pull of gravity on Earth than on the Moon?

3

ARTIFICIAL

WAXING

Earth, Sun & Moon

Unit 5E

1 Describe the **relationship** between length of **day** and **night** in Britain in **Summer**

2 Why is the temperature **warmer in Summer** than in **Winter**?

Science Chatterbox 7

PHASE

5 Describe **two ways** the **Earth** is **moving in space**

in Summer, Britain is tilted **towards** the Sun, so days are **longer** and nights are **shorter**

in Summer, the Sun shines for a **longer period** and from a **higher angle,** the rays are **more concentrated**

because it is **highest** in the sky at this time, nearly **directly overhead**

6 Why does the Sun cast a **shorter shadow** around **midday**?

spinning on its axis & **orbiting** around the sun

the Sun **rises in the east**, so shadows point **towards** the **opposite direction, west**.

because the **position** and **angle** of the Sun - **changes** through the day

Which **direction** do shadows **point towards**, at **8.00 am**?

© Chris Jones 2008

in Winter, Britain is TILTED AWAY FROM the Sun, so days are shorter & nights are longer

because - from a full Moon, through all the different phases, back to the next full Moon - takes 28 days

Why do the **length** and **position** of shadows **change** during the day?

8

7

WANING

4 Describe the relationship, between **length** of **day** and **night** during the **winter**, in Britain

What evidence do we have, that the Moon takes **28 days,** for a **complete orbit** of the **Earth**?

3

ECLIPSE

© Chris Jones 2008

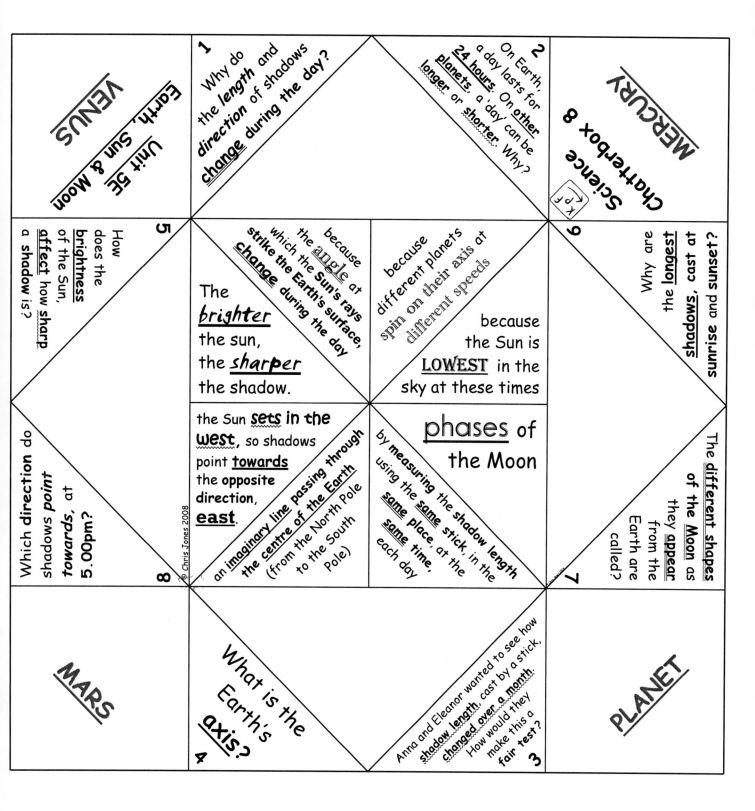

1 Why do the *length* and *direction* of shadows **change** during the day?

2 On Earth, a day lasts for **24 hours**. On **other planets**, a 'day' can be **longer** or **shorter**. Why?

Science Chatterbox 8

MERCURY

VENUS

Unit 5E Earth, Sun & Moon

5 How does the **brightness** of the Sun, **affect** how **sharp** a shadow is?

because the **angle** at which the **Sun's rays** **strike** the Earth's surface, **change** during the day

The **brighter** the sun, the **sharper** the shadow.

because different planets spin on their axis at different speeds

because the Sun is **LOWEST** in the sky at these times

6 Why are the **longest** **shadows**, cast at sunrise and sunset?

Which **direction** do shadows *point* **towards**, at 5.00pm?

the Sun **sets in the west**, so shadows point **towards** the opposite direction, **east**.

© Chris Jones 2008

an **imaginary** line passing through **the centre of the Earth** (from the North Pole to the South Pole)

phases of the Moon

by **measuring** the shadow length using the **same** stick, in the **same** place, at the **same** time, each day

The **different shapes** of the **Moon** as they **appear** from the Earth are called?

7

MARS

What is the Earth's **axis**? **4**

Anna and Eleanor wanted to see how **shadow length**, cast by a stick, **changed over a month**. How would they make this a **fair test**? **3**

PLANET

SATURN

Earth, Sun & Moon
Unit 5E

1 What **holds** the **solar system in place**, preventing the planets from flying off into deep space?

2 the Sun is a giant ball of exploding and burning gas. **Which gas?**

Science Chatterbox 9

JUPITER

5 Why does the Moon **appear** **to change shape?** (even though we know it's a sphere)

the **pull** of **gravity** from the **Sun**

the Sun **shines** on it from **different angles**, so *we see* **different amounts** of sunlight, falling on it

hydrogen (its temperature in the **centre** is 15 million **degrees centigrade**!)

the Earth is **held in place** by the **pull of the Sun's gravity**

6 What **holds** the **Earth in place** during its orbit around the Sun?

there is *no air in space*, therefore there is **no air resistance** (friction)

© Chris Jones 2008

astronomy, GPS Systems telecommunications, weather tracking, spying, etc

An **elliptical path** (a kind of *slightly squashed circle*)

when the Moon is **BETWEEN** the Earth and Sun, it **blocks** the Sun for a few minutes casting a shadow onto the Earth

What **shape** is the **path** that the Earth takes around the **Sun?** (its orbit)

8 Why has the Earth been orbiting the Sun for billions of years, without *slowing down?*

NEPTUNE

4 What kind of uses do man-made satellites which orbit the Earth, have?

3 Explain what occurs during a **solar eclipse**

7

URANUS

© Chris Jones 2008

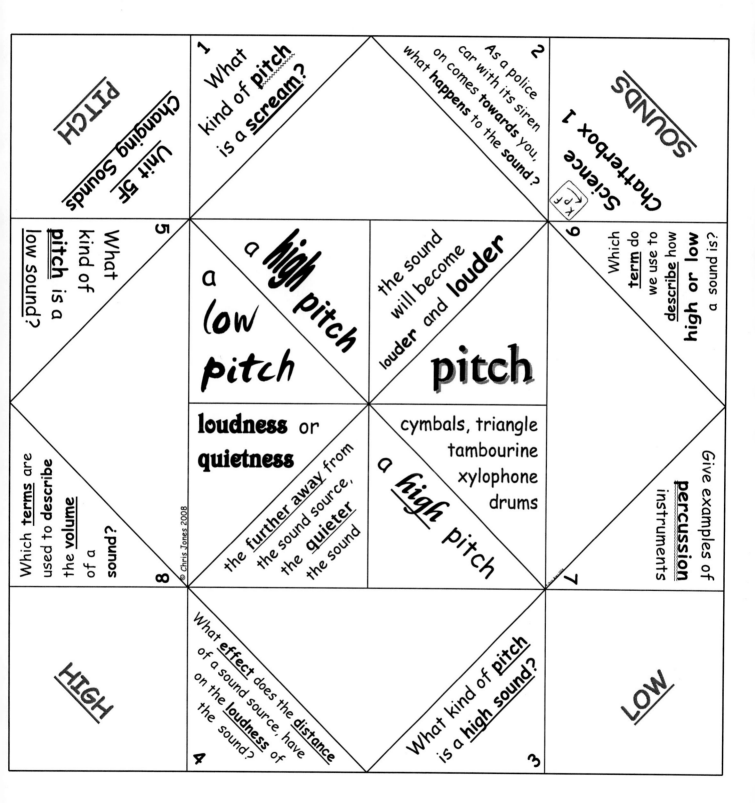

PITCH

Unit 5F Changing Sounds

1 What kind of **pitch** is a **scream**?

2 As a police car with its siren on comes **towards** you, what **happens** to the **sound**?

SOUNDS

Science Chatterbox 1

Which **term** do we use to describe how **high or low** a sound is? 6

5 What kind of **pitch** is a low sound?

a **high** pitch

a **low** pitch

the sound will become louder and **louder**

pitch

© Chris Jones 2008

loudness or quietness

the **further away** from the sound source, the **quieter** the sound

cymbals, triangle tambourine xylophone drums

a **high** pitch

8 Which **terms** are used to describe the **volume** of a **sound**?

Give examples of **percussion** instruments 7

HIGH

4 What **effect** does the **distance** of a sound source, have on the **loudness** of the sound?

What kind of **pitch** is a **high sound**? 3

LOW

© Chris Jones 2008

Unit 5F

Changing Sounds

Chatterbox 2   Level 3

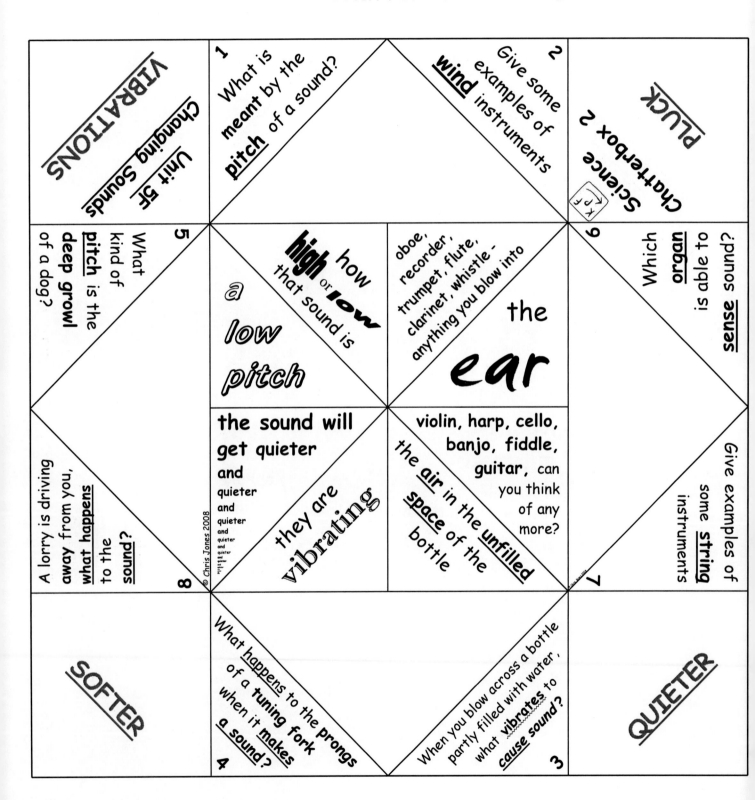

VIBRATIONS

Changing Sounds

Unit 5F

1 What is meant by the **pitch** of a sound?

2 Give some examples of **wind** instruments

PLUCK

Science Chatterbox 2

5 What kind of **pitch** is the **deep growl** of a dog?

how **high** or **low** that sound is

a **low pitch**

oboe, recorder, trumpet, flute, clarinet, whistle - anything you blow into

the **ear**

6 Which **organ** is able to **sense sound**?

the sound will get quieter and quieter and quieter and quieter and quieter......

© Chris Jones 2008

they are **vibrating**

violin, harp, cello, banjo, fiddle, guitar, can you think of any more?

the **air** in the **unfilled space** of the bottle

Give examples of some **string** instruments

A lorry is driving away from you, what **happens** to the **sound**?

8

SOFTER

4 What **happens** to the prongs of a **tuning fork** when it **makes a sound**?

7

When you blow across a bottle partly filled with water, what **vibrates** to **cause sound**? 3

QUIETER

© Chris Jones 2008

Unit 5F

Changing Sounds

Chatterbox 3   Level 4

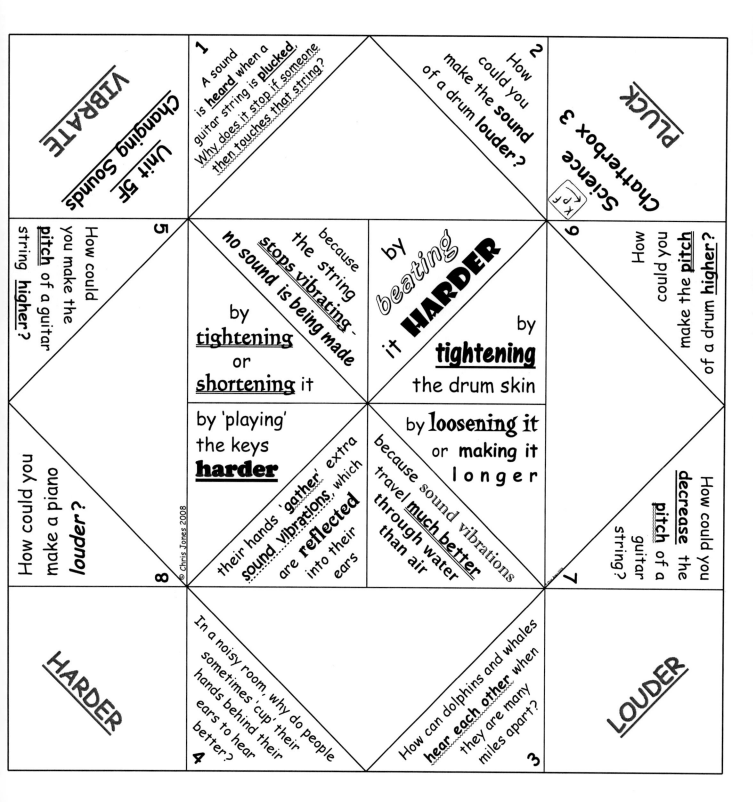

VIBRATE

Unit 5F Changing Sounds

1 A sound is **heard** when a guitar string is **plucked**. Why does it stop if someone then touches that string?

2 How could you make the **sound** of a drum louder?

Science Chatterbox 3

PLUCK

5 How could you make the **pitch** of a guitar string **higher**?

because the string **stops vibrating** - no sound is being made

by **tightening** or **shortening** it

by **beating** it **HARDER**

by **tightening** the drum skin

6 How could you make the **pitch** of a drum **higher**?

by 'playing' the keys **harder**

their hands 'gather' extra **sound vibrations**, which are **reflected** into their ears

by **loosening it** or **making it longer**

because sound vibrations travel **much better** through water than air

7 How could you **decrease** the **pitch** of a guitar string?

How could you make a piano **louder**?

HARDER

8

© Chris Jones 2008

4 In a noisy room, why do people sometimes 'cup' their hands behind their ears to hear better?

3 How can dolphins and whales **hear each other** when they are many miles apart?

LOUDER

© Chris Jones 2008

51

TIGHTER

Unit 5F Changing Sounds

1 If you put your fingers on your throat, then **hum** loudly, what can you feel?

2 Which is the odd one out: the sound of a fog horn, a cow mooing, a mouse squeaking or a bass drum?

Science Chatterbox 4

DRUMSKIN

5 What happens if you put rice grains on a drum, then hit it?

You can feel your throat **vibrating**

the grains start **jumping** around because the drum skin is **vibrating**

the squeaking mouse is the only **high pitched sound** - the others are low pitched

sound is caused when **objects vibrate**

6 What **causes sound?**

smooth or **hard** surfaces

a cat purring has a **quiet volume**, the others have **loud volumes**

materials that **absorb sound vibrations** - because fewer vibrations reach your ears- sound is quieter

the drum skin **vibrates**, causing the **air to vibrate** -these **vibrations** then travel to your ear

7 What is a **sound insulator?**

8 Which kind of surface does sound **reflect** ('bounce') off?

© Chris Jones 2008

HIGHER

4 Which is the odd one out: a jet engine, a cat purring, a road drill or 100 children at playtime?

3 How does **sound travel** from a drum to your ear?

PITCH

© Chris Jones 2008

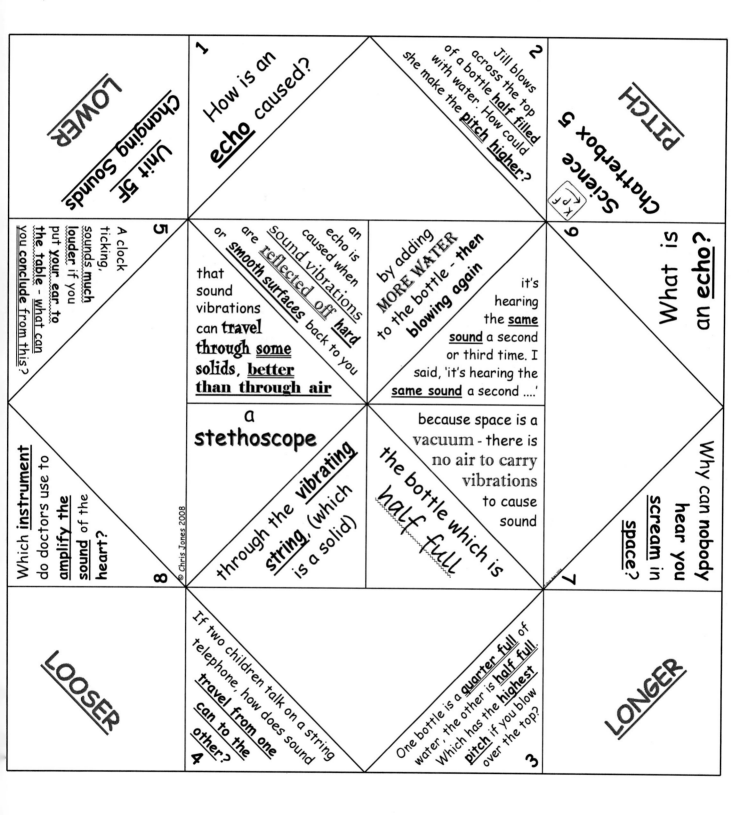

LOWER

Unit 5F Changing Sounds

1 — How is an **echo** caused?

2 — Jill blows across the top of a bottle **half filled** with water. How could she make the **pitch higher**?

PITCH

Science Chatterbox 5

5 — A clock ticking, **sounds much louder** if you put **your ear** to the table – **what can you conclude from this?**

an echo is caused when **sound vibrations** are **reflected off hard** or **smooth surfaces** back to you

that sound vibrations can **travel through some** solids, **better than through air**

by adding **MORE WATER** to the bottle – **then blowing again**

it's hearing the **same sound** a second or third time. I said, 'it's hearing the **same sound** a second ....'

6 — What is an **echo**?

Which **instrument** do doctors use to **amplify the sound** of the heart?

a **stethoscope**

through the **vibrating string** (which is a solid)

the bottle which is **half full**

because space is a vacuum - there is no air to carry vibrations to cause sound

Why can nobody hear you **scream** in **space?**

8 — © Chris Jones 2008

LOOSER

4 — If two children talk on a string telephone, how does sound **travel from one can to the other?**

3 — One bottle is a **quarter full** of water, the other is **half full**. Which has the **highest pitch** if you blow over the top?

7 — LONGER

Unit 5F

Changing Sounds

Chatterbox 6   Level 5

VOLUME

Changing Sounds

Unit 5F

1 What **effect** does the **thickness** of a guitar string, **have on** the **pitch**, when you pluck it?

2 What **effect** does **changing** the **length** of a guitar string have on the **pitch**?

Science Chatterbox 6

DECIBEL

5 What **effect** does tightening a guitar string have on the pitch?

the **tighter** the string, the **higher** the pitch

the **thicker** the string, the **lower** the **pitch**; thinner the **string**, higher the **pitch**

the **shorter** the string, the **higher** the **pitch**, the **longer** the string, the **lower** the pitch

the **HARDER** you beat a drum, the **LOUDER** it sounds

6 How does the **force used** to **beat** a drum - **affect** the volume?

the **thickness**, the **length** and how **tight** it is stretched

the **looser** the string, the **lower** the pitch

tighter the skin the **higher** the **pitch**

the **HARDER** a string is **plucked**, the **LOUDER** the **sound** that is made

How does the **amount** that a drum skin is **tightened affect the pitch**?

8 Which three things could **affect** the **pitch** of a guitar string?

© Chris Jones 2008

7

FREQUENCY

4 What **effect** does loosening a guitar string have **on the pitch**?

What **effect** does the **force** used to pluck a string, **have on the volume**? **3**

ECHO

54

© Chris Jones 2008

CYMBALS

Changing Sounds

Unit 5F

PERCUSSION

Science Chatterbox 7

1 Which type of materials make GOOD sound insulators?

2 The answer is; **the looser the string, the lower the pitch.** What was the question?

5 The answer is; **'the harder you beat a drum, the louder it sounds'.** What was the question?

materials with **soft surfaces,** like cotton, wool and cloth because these **absorb sound**

How does the **force used** to **beat** a drum, **affect** the volume?

What **effect** does **loosening** a guitar string have on the **pitch**?

6 The answer is; **'guitar, violin, cello, banjo'.** What was the question?

Give **examples** of instruments which have **strings** that **vibrate**

Which **3** variables can **affect** the **pitch** of a guitar string?

© Chris Jones 2008

What **effect** does the **force used** to **pluck** a string, have on the **volume?**

How does the **thickness** of a string **affect** the pitch?

How does **tightening** a drum skin **affect** the **pitch?**

The answer is; **the thicker the string, the lower the pitch.** What was the question?

7

8 The answer is; **the thickness, length and how tight it is stretched'.** What was the question?

TAMBOURINE

The answer is; **'the harder you pluck a string, the louder the sound** - what was the question?

4

The answer is; **'the tighter the skin, the higher the pitch'. What was the question?**

3

XYLOPHONE

VIOLA

Unit 5F Changing Sounds

1 In some cowboy films, a person may put their ear to the railway track to listen for the train. **Why?**

2 The <u>number</u> of **times** a sound wave **vibrates** each second is called?

Science Chatterbox 8

STRING

5 How do we know that <u>light</u> **travels** faster than <u>sound</u>?

because the sound vibrations of the train **travel** through metal <u>better</u> than through air

the frequency

(dB) decibels

6 Which unit of measure is used to record loudness?

because, for example, we can **SEE** the **lightning** <u>BEFORE</u> we **HEAR** the **thunder**

about **600mph (miles per hour)**

because **very loud** sounds can <u>damage</u> ears and cause loss of **hearing**

the **looser** the **skin**, the **lower** the **pitch**

the **hammer**, **anvil** and **stirrup**

7 What <u>effect</u> does <u>loosening</u> a drum skin, have on the <u>pitch</u>?

© Chris Jones 2008

8 How <u>fast</u> does **sound travel** at sea level?

CELLO

4 Why do we need <u>insulation</u> **against** some very **loud sounds**, like a pneumatic drill?

Which are the <u>three bones</u> in your <u>ear</u> that help to <u>amplify</u> any sounds entering? **3**

GUITAR

© Chris Jones 2008

CHAIN

Unit 6A Interdependence and Adaptation

1 What is the **function** of the **stem**?

2 What is usually used to **represent** the feeding relationships in a **habitat**?

FOOD

Science Chatterbox 1

6 What do green plants **need** to **grow well**?

5 What do we call the **place** where an organism **lives**?

to **support** the plant and to **transport** water and food **through** the plant

a **habitat**

prey

a **food chain**

air
light
water
and **warmth**

to **make food** for the plant

What is the main **function** of the **leaves**?

An animal that is **hunted** and **eaten** by another animal is called?

an animal that **HUNTS** and **EATS** other animals

to **anchor** the plant and **take in nutrients** and **water**

7

© Chris Jones 2008

RELATIONSHIP

What is a **predator**?

4

What is the **function** of the **roots**?

3

WEB

© Chris Jones 2008

Unit 6A   Interdependence and Adaptation

Chatterbox 2   Level 3

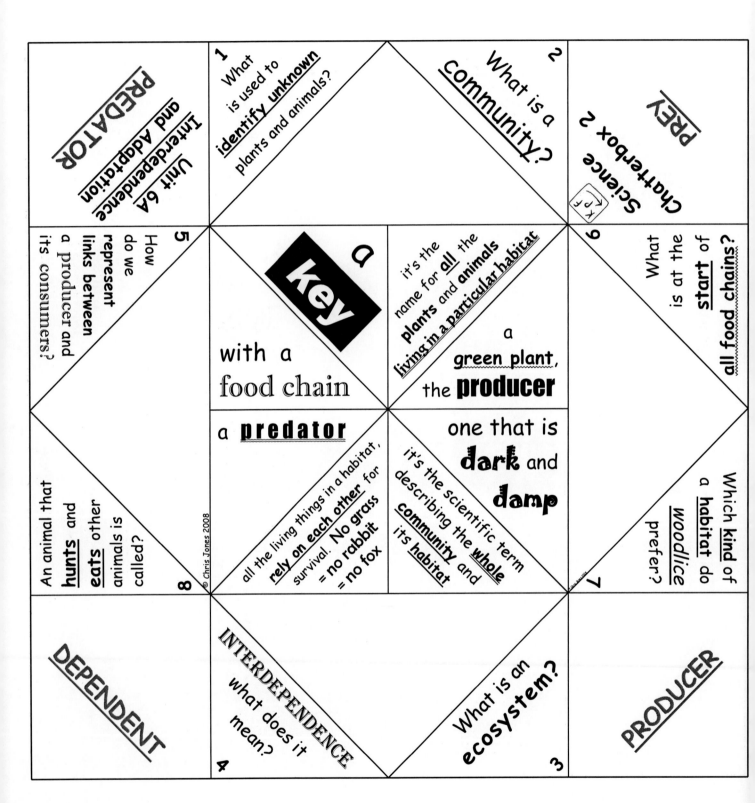

PREDATOR

Unit 6A Interdependence and Adaptation

1 What is used to identify **unknown** plants and animals?

What is a **community**?

2

Science Chatterbox 2

PREY

5 How do we represent links between a producer and its consumers?

a **key**

with a food chain

a **predator**

it's the name for **all** the **plants** and **animals** living in a particular habitat

a green plant, the **producer**

one that is **dark** and **damp**

What is at the **start** of all food chains?

6

An animal that **hunts** and **eats** other animals is called?

© Chris Jones 2008

8

all the living things in a habitat, **rely on each other** for survival. No grass = no rabbit = no fox

it's the scientific term describing the whole **community** and its **habitat**

Which **kind** of a **habitat** do *woodlice* prefer?

7

PRODUCER

DEPENDENT

INTERDEPENDENCE what does it mean?

4

What is an **ecosystem**?

3

© Chris Jones 2008

Unit 6A Interdependence and Adaptation

Chatterbox 3   Level 4

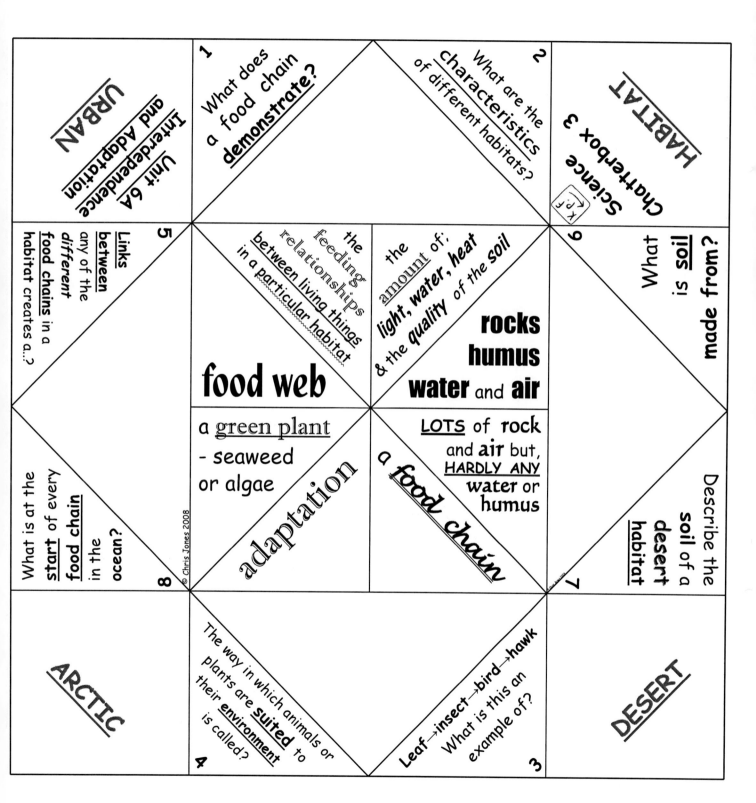

1 What does a food chain **demonstrate?**

2 What are the **characteristics** of different habitats?

Unit 6A **Interdependence and Adaptation**

URBAN

Science **Chatterbox 3**

HABITAT

5 **Links** between any of the different **food chains** in a habitat creates a..?

the **feeding** **relationships** between living things in a particular habitat

the **amount** of: **light, water, heat** & the **quality** of the soil

rocks **humus** **water** and **air**

food web

a **green plant** - seaweed or algae

adaptation

a **food chain**

LOTS of **rock** and **air** but, **HARDLY ANY** water or humus

What is **soil** made from?

Describe the **soil** of a **desert** **habitat**

What is at the **start** of every **food chain** in the ocean?

© Chris Jones 2008

8

ARCTIC

4 The way in which animals or plants are **suited** to their **environment** is called?

Leaf→insect→bird→hawk What is this an example of?

3

DESERT

7

Unit 6A   Interdependence and Adaptation

Chatterbox 4   Level 4

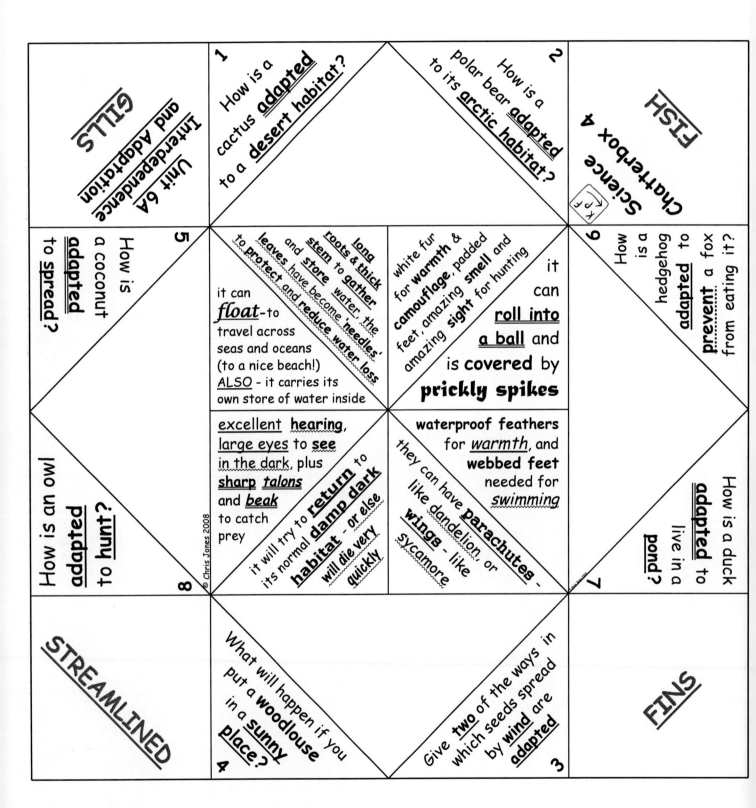

GILLS

Unit 6A Interdependence and Adaptation

1 How is a cactus **adapted** to a **desert habitat?**

2 How is a polar bear **adapted** to its **arctic habitat?**

Science Chatterbox 4

FISH

5 How is a coconut **adapted** to **spread?**

long roots & thick stem to gather and **store** water, the leaves have become 'needles' to **protect** and **reduce water loss**

it can **float** - to travel across seas and oceans (to a nice beach!) ALSO - it carries its own store of water inside

white fur for **warmth** & **camouflage**, padded feet, amazing **smell** and amazing **sight** for hunting

it can **roll into a ball** and is **covered** by **prickly spikes**

6 How is a hedgehog **adapted** to **prevent** a fox from eating it?

excellent **hearing**, **large eyes** to **see** in the dark, plus **sharp talons** and **beak** to catch prey

© Chris Jones 2008

it will try to **return** to its normal **damp dark habitat** - or else will die very quickly

waterproof feathers for **warmth**, and **webbed feet** needed for **swimming**

they can have **parachutes** - like dandelion, or **wings** - like sycamore

How is a duck **adapted** to live in a **pond?**

8 How is an owl **adapted** to **hunt?**

STREAMLINED

4 What will happen if you put a **woodlouse** in a **sunny place?**

3 Give **two** of the ways in which seeds spread by **wind** are **adapted**

FINS

© Chris Jones 2008

Unit 6A Interdependence and Adaptation

Chatterbox 5   Level 4

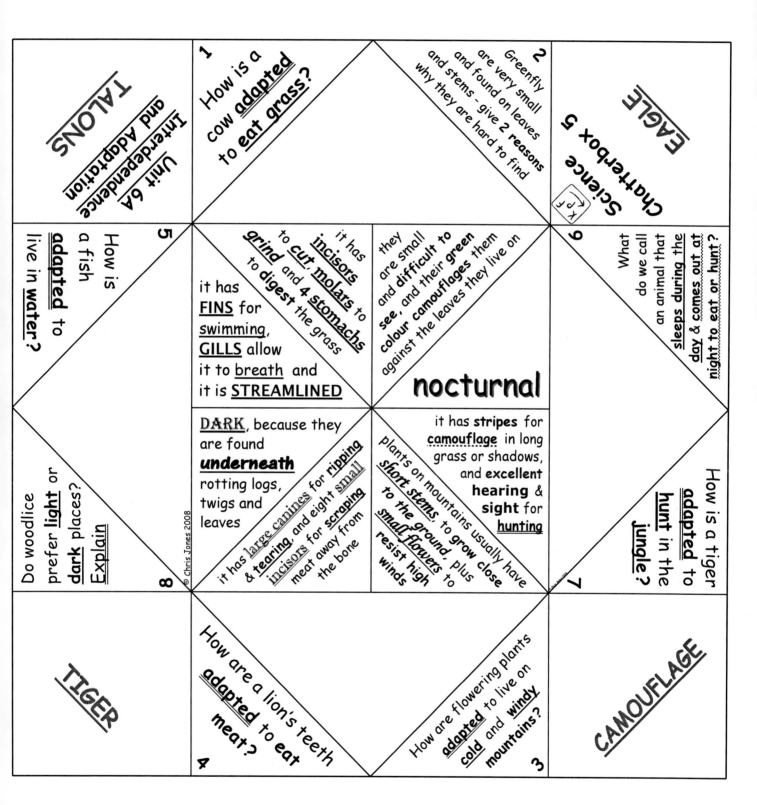

TALONS

Unit 6A Interdependence and Adaptation

1 How is a cow **adapted** to **eat grass?**

2 Greenfly are very small and found on leaves and stems - give 2 reasons why they are hard to find

Science Chatterbox 5

EAGLE

5 How is a fish **adapted** to live in **water?**

it has **incisors** to **cut**, **molars** to **grind** and **4 stomachs** to **digest** the grass

it has **FINS** for **swimming**, **GILLS** allow it to **breath** and it is **STREAMLINED**

they are small and difficult to **see**, and their **green** colour **camouflages** them against the leaves they live on

6 What do we call an animal that **sleeps during the day & comes out at night to eat or hunt?**

nocturnal

Do woodlice prefer **light** or **dark** places? **Explain**

DARK, because they are found **underneath** rotting logs, twigs and leaves

© Chris Jones 2008

it has **large canines** for **ripping & tearing**, and eight **small incisors** for **scraping** meat away from the bone

plants on mountains usually have **short stems**, to grow close to the ground, plus **small flowers** to resist high winds

it has **stripes** for **camouflage** in long grass or shadows, and **excellent hearing & sight** for **hunting**

How is a tiger **adapted** to **hunt** in the **jungle?** 7

TIGER

4 How are a lion's teeth **adapted** to **eat meat?**

How are flowering plants **adapted** to live on **cold** and **windy** mountains? 3

CAMOUFLAGE

© Chris Jones 2008

Unit 6A — Interdependence and Adaptation

Chatterbox 6   Level 5

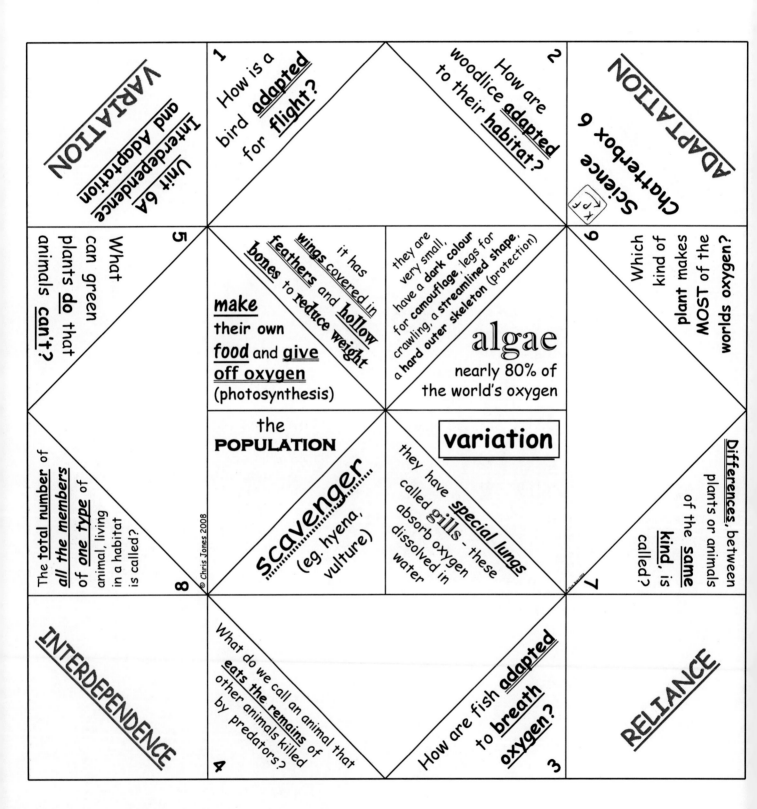

VARIATION — Unit 6A Interdependence and Adaptation

1. How is a bird **adapted** for **flight**?

2. How are woodlice **adapted** to their **habitat**?

ADAPTATION — Science Chatterbox 6

5. What can green plants **do** that animals **can't**?

it has **wings** covered in **feathers** and **hollow** **bones** to reduce weight

make their own **food** and **give off oxygen** (photosynthesis)

they are very small, have a **dark colour** for **camouflage**, legs for crawling, a streamlined shape, a **hard outer** skeleton (protection)

6. Which kind of plant makes **MOST** of the world's oxygen?

algae
nearly 80% of the world's oxygen

the **POPULATION**

variation

they have **special lungs** called **gills** – these absorb oxygen dissolved in water

Differences, between plants or animals of the **same** **kind**, is called?

The total number of **all the members** of **one type** of animal, living in a habitat is called?

© Chris Jones 2008

scavenger (eg. hyena, vulture)

8.

7.

INTERDEPENDENCE

4. What do we call an animal that **eats the remains** of other animals killed by predators?

3. How are fish **adapted** to **breath oxygen**?

RELIANCE

© Chris Jones 2008

Unit 6A Interdependence and Adaptation

Chatterbox 7   Level 5

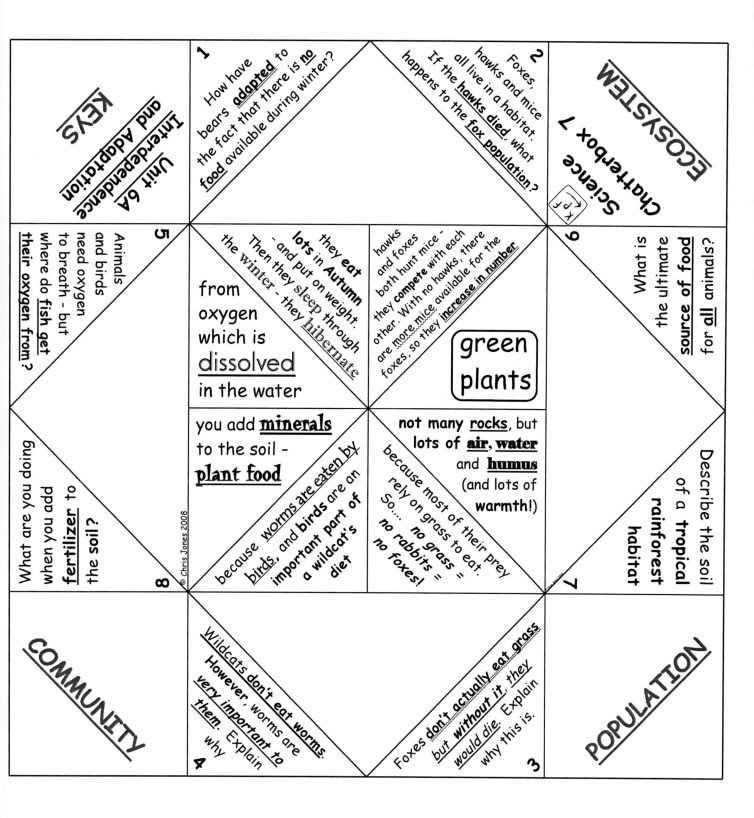

KEYS

Unit 6A Interdependence and Adaptation

1 How have bears **adapted** to the fact that there is **no** **food** available during winter?

2 Foxes, hawks and mice all live in a habitat. If the **hawks died**, what happens to the **fox population**?

Science Chatterbox 7

ECOSYSTEM

5 Animals and birds need oxygen to breath - but where do **fish get** **their oxygen from**?

they **eat** **lots** in **Autumn** - and put on weight. Then they sleep through the winter - they **hibernate**

from oxygen which is **dissolved** in the water

hawks and foxes both hunt mice - they **compete** with each other. With no hawks, there are **more mice** available for the foxes, so they **increase in number**

6 What is the ultimate **source of food** for **all animals**?

green plants

you add **minerals** to the soil - **plant food**

because **worms are eaten by** **birds**, and **birds** are an **important part of** **a wildcat's diet**

not many **rocks**, but lots of **air**, **water** and **humus** (and lots of warmth!)

because most of their prey rely on grass to eat. So.... **no grass** = **no rabbits** = **no foxes!**

Describe the soil of a **tropical** **rainforest** **habitat**

© Chris Jones 2008

What are you doing when you add **fertilizer** to the soil?

8

COMMUNITY

4 Wildcats don't eat worms. However, worms are very important to them. Explain why

Foxes **don't actually eat grass** but **without it, they** **would die**. Explain why this is.

3

POPULATION

Unit 6B

Micro-organisms

Chatterbox 1   Level 3

GERMS

Micro-organisms Unit 6B

1 What causes **bad breath?**

2 Why should you **wash** your **hands before** preparing or touching food?

Science Chatterbox 1

MICROBES

5 How can micro-organisms be **harmful** to humans?

bacteria living in your mouth!!! ☹

by causing **disease** and **illnesses**

it's **hygienic** -it removes any **harmful micro-** organisms from your hands

plaque

6 What do we call **bacteria** that *cause* **tooth decay?**

What is meant by the term 'germs'?

it's the name we usually use for **micro-organisms** that **cause** **disease** & **illness**

© Chris Jones 2008

a **microscope**

food, water warmth oxygen

food production, decaying dead plants and animals, making some **medicines** and **helping** our **digestion** in

7 What do micro-organisms **need to grow?**

BACTERIA

4 What is the special instrument that scientists use to **look** at micro-organisms?

Give **four ways** in which **micro-organisms** are **helpful** to humans **3**

VIRUS

© Chris Jones 2008

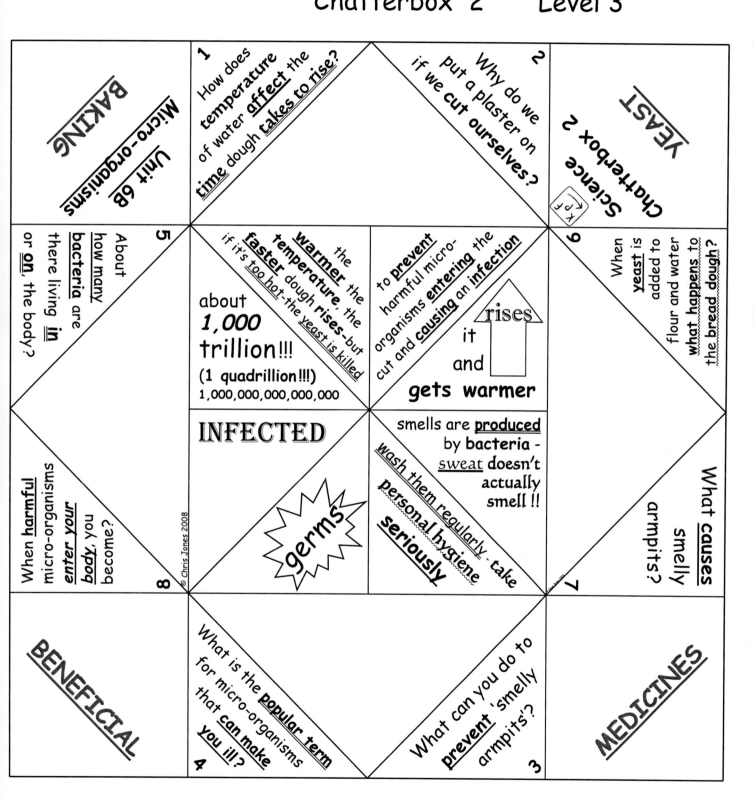

BAKING

Micro-organisms

Unit 6B

1 How does temperature of water **affect** the time dough <u>takes to rise</u>?

2 Why do we put a plaster on if we **cut ourselves**?

Science Chatterbox 2

YEAST

About **how many** <u>bacteria</u> are there living <u>in</u> or <u>on</u> the body? **5**

the **warmer** the temperature, the **faster** dough **rises** - but if it's too hot - <u>the yeast is killed</u>

about **1,000 trillion!!!** (1 quadrillion!!!) 1,000,000,000,000,000

to **prevent** harmful micro- organisms **entering** the cut and **causing** an <u>infection</u>

rises it and **gets warmer**

6 When <u>yeast</u> is added to flour and water <u>what happens to the bread dough</u>?

INFECTED

smells are <u>produced</u> by **bacteria** - <u>sweat</u> doesn't actually smell !!

germs

wash them regularly - take **personal hygiene** <u>seriously</u>

When **harmful** micro-organisms <u>enter your body</u>, you become? **8**

© Chris Jones 2008

What <u>causes</u> smelly armpits?

BENEFICIAL

What is the **popular term** for micro-organisms that **can make** <u>you ill</u>? **4**

What can you do to **prevent** 'smelly armpits'? **3**

MEDICINES

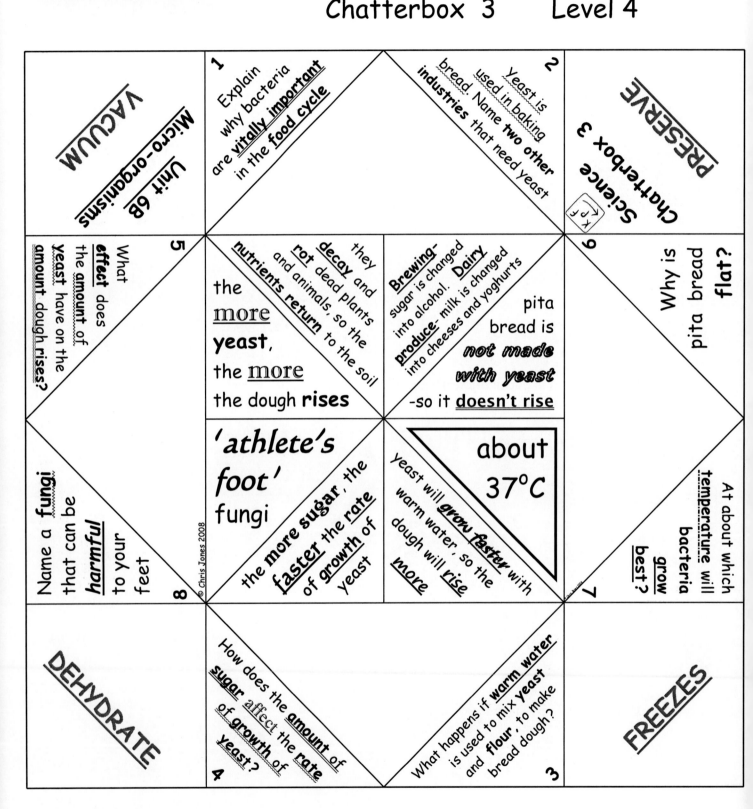

VACUUM

Micro-organisms

Unit 6B

1 Explain why bacteria are **vitally important** in the **food cycle**

2 **Yeast is** used in baking bread. Name **two** other industries that need yeast

Science Chatterbox 3

PRESERVE

5 What **effect** does the **amount of yeast** have on the **amount dough rises?**

they **decay** and **rot** dead plants and animals, so the **nutrients return** to the soil

the **more** **yeast**, the **more** the dough **rises**

Brewing- sugar is changed into alcohol. **Dairy produce**- milk is changed into cheeses and yoghurts

pita bread is *not made with yeast* -so it **doesn't rise**

6 Why is pita bread flat?

Name a **fungi** that can be **harmful** to your feet

'athlete's foot' fungi

© Chris Jones 2008

the **more sugar**, the **faster** the rate of **growth** of yeast

yeast will **grow faster** with warm water, so the dough will **rise** **more**

about 37°C

At about which **temperature** will bacteria **grow best?**

8

DEHYDRATE

How does the **amount of sugar** **affect** the **rate** of **growth** of yeast?

What happens if **warm water** is used to mix **yeast** and **flour**, to make bread dough?

7

FREEZES

4

3

© Chris Jones 2008

Unit 6B

Micro-organisms

Chatterbox 4   Level 4

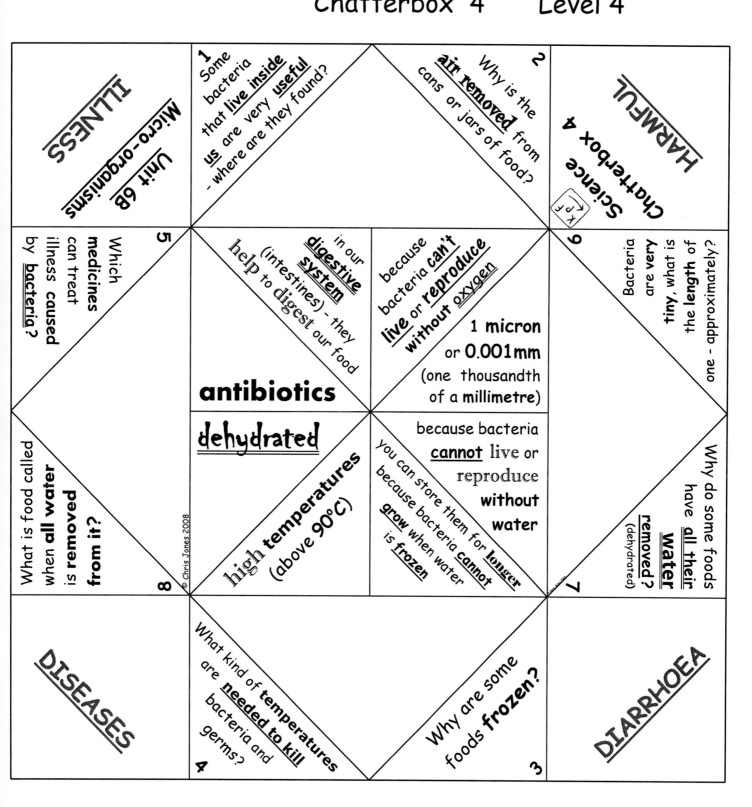

ILLNESS

Micro-organisms

Unit 6B

1 Some bacteria that **live inside** us are very **useful** - where are they found?

2 Why is the **air removed** from cans or jars of food?

Science Chatterbox 4

HARMFUL

Bacteria are very tiny, what is the **length of** one - approximately?

5 Which **medicines** can treat illness caused by **bacteria**?

in our **digestive system** (intestines) - they help to digest our food

because bacteria **can't live** or **reproduce without oxygen**

1 micron or 0.001mm (one thousandth of a millimetre)

6

Why do some foods have **all their water removed?** (dehydrated)

antibiotics

dehydrated

because bacteria **cannot** live or reproduce **without water**

You can store them for **longer** because bacteria **cannot grow** when water is **frozen**

What is food called when **all water** is removed **from it?**

high **temperatures** (above 90°C)

© Chris Jones 2008

8

7

DISEASES

What kind of **temperatures** are **needed to kill** bacteria and germs?

4

Why are some foods **frozen?**

3

DIARRHOEA

© Chris Jones 2008

PENICILLIN

Micro-organisms

Unit 6B

FLEMING

Science Chatterbox 5

1 If your body is able to **protect** **itself** against a **particular** disease, it is said to be...?

2 Which **scientist** **discovered** that **antiseptics** could **kill** **bacteria** - so patients having operations didn't get infected?

5 Which **scientist** discovered how **vaccination** (the 'jab') helps prevent some **diseases**?

an English doctor named **Edward Jenner** (1749-1823)

immune

an English surgeon named **Joseph Lister** (1827-1912)

a French chemist named **Louis Pasteur** (1822-1895)

6 Which **scientist** discovered that **decay** is **caused** by **bacteria**?

a Scottish doctor - **Alexander Fleming** (1881-1955)

Antony van Leeuwenhoek - a Dutch scientist (1632-1723)

© Chris Jones 2008

get **vaccinated** (have a jab!)

Pasteurization - discovered by **Louis Pasteur**

8 Penicillin is a useful medicine for **killing** **bacteria**. Who discovered it?

7 What is the usual way to **prevent** **infection** from a **virus**?

PASTEURISATION

4 Which **scientist** was the first to **observe bacteria** through a **microscope**?

3 What is the process of **killing** **bacteria** with **heat** to **preserve food** called?

PASTEUR

© Chris Jones 2008

Unit 6B

Micro-organisms

Chatterbox 6   Level 5

JENNER · Micro-organisms · Unit 6B

1 Explain how **freezing** foods can help to **preserve** them

2 What **causes** bread dough to **rise?**

Science Chatterbox 6

VACCINATION

5 When you have a 'jab' – what is **actually** being **injected** into you?

microbes can't **grow** in very **cold temperatures**, so the food doesn't start rotting

yeast is growing and producing **carbon dioxide** (CO_2), which is trapped as 'bubbles' in the dough

without water, it's **impossible** for microbes to **grow** and **reproduce**

6 Explain why cereals are usually **dehydrated** (all the water is removed)

dead viruses so if you get infected by the living virus later on - your body **recognises** & **fights** it **immediately**

it is **KILLED** by the **HIGH** temperature (once its job is done!)

© Chris Jones 2008

to help **preserve** the food, - bacteria is unable to **reproduce** or **grow** without air

hot temperatures and **lack of air** will **kill** any microbes

in the **freezer**, because it's too **cold** for bacteria to **GROW** - any water is **frozen solid**

Give **two** ways in which **canning** food **kills bacteria** (putting food into tins)

8 What happens to **yeast** during **baking?**

IMMUNISATION

4 Explain why **air** is **removed**, creating a **vacuum**, in some packaged foods, e.g. jars of jam

3 In a kitchen, where's the **best place** to **store** bread - to stop it going **mouldy?**

JAB

Unit 6B

Micro-organisms

Chatterbox 7   Level 5

LISTER

Micro-organisms

Unit 6B

1 **Before** an operation, the surgeon's knife is **sterilized** - what does this mean?

2 Bacteria reproduce by **dividing** every 30 **minutes**. How many could **reproduce** in 24 hours? - starting with just a single one!

STERILIZATION

Science Chatterbox 7

5 Which two **precautions** do scientists usually take when experimenting with bacteria?

all bacteria or germs are **killed** to **prevent** any **infection** (sterile means 'without life')

they wear **gloves** and a **face mask**

with the *right conditions*, **300,000 billion** (281,474,976,710,656) - to be precise!

disinfectant (like bleach)

6 Which liquid is **put** used to keep kitchen work surfaces free from **micro-organisms**?

flu (influenza), polio, diphtheria mumps, a cold chicken pox measles

rhinoviruses

to **check** the **results** or to see if some people might have a **bad reaction**

food poisoning, diarrhoea, toothache, cholera, **tuberculosis**

© Chris Jones 2008

Name a few illnesses **caused** by a **virus**

8

Why do doctors **test new drugs** on **many** people, not just **one**?

7

HYGIENIC

Several viruses can cause the **symptoms** of a 'cold' - what is the main one responsible?

4

Name a few illnesses **caused** by **bacteria**

3

INFECTION

© Chris Jones 2008

Unit 6C

More About Dissolving

Chatterbox 1   Level 3

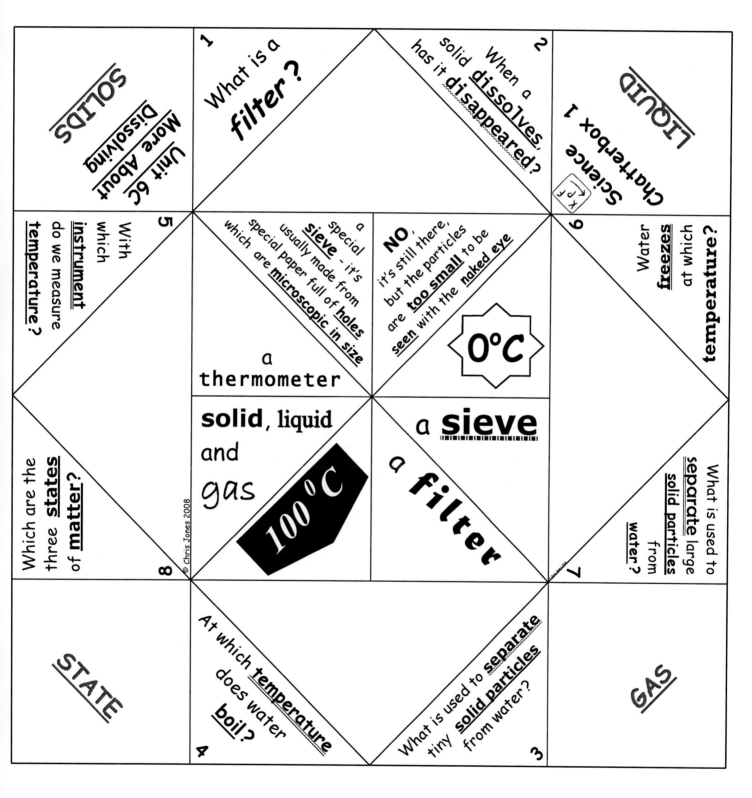

SOLIDS

Unit 6C
More About
Dissolving

1 What is a **filter?**

2 When a solid **dissolves,** has it **disappeared?**

Science Chatterbox 1

LIQUID

5 With which **instrument** do we measure **temperature?**

a special **sieve** - it's usually made from special paper full of holes which are **microscopic in size**

NO, it's still there, but the particles are **too small** to be seen with the **naked eye**

0°C

Water **freezes** at which **temperature?**

a thermometer

solid, liquid and gas

a **sieve**

100°C

a **filter**

What is used to **separate** large **solid particles** from **water?**

Which are the three **states** of **matter?**

8

© Chris Jones 2008

7

At which **temperature** does water **boil?**

4

What is used to **separate** tiny **solid particles** from water?

3

STATE

GAS

© Chris Jones 2008

Unit 6C

More About Dissolving

Chatterbox 2   Level 3

HOLES

Unit 6C
More About
Dissolving

1 Which equipment could be used to separate sand from water?

2 How could Ruby separate a mixture of sugar and rice?

FILTER

Science
Chatterbox 2

5 How could you separate a goldfish from water?

a funnel with filter paper - pour the mixture in - the sand remains in the filter paper

she could use a sieve - the sugar goes through, but the rice remains in the sieve

6 What happens when salt is put into hot water?

use a net - it's a sieve

it DISSOLVES very quickly

evaporation

evaporating the water to leave the salt behind

Name the process where a dissolved solid can be separated from water?

8

© Chris Jones 2008

a tea bag acts as a filter, letting flavour through, (dissolved), but not the leaves (solid)

the hotter the water, the faster the rate a soluble solid will dissolve

Olga dissolves some rock salt in water - how could she get the salt back?

7

MICROSCOPIC

4 What is used to prevent your cup filling with tea leaves?

3 What effect does temperature of water have on the rate a soluble solid will dissolve?

EVAPORATES

© Chris Jones 2008

Unit 6C

More About Dissolving

Chatterbox 3   Level 4

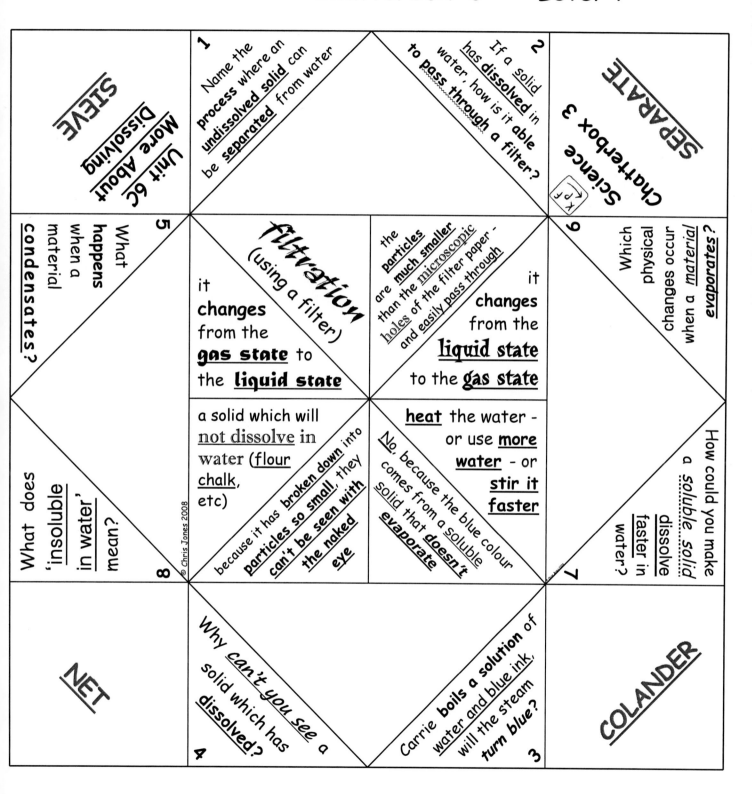

SIEVE

Unit 6C More About Dissolving

1 Name the process where an undissolved solid can be separated from water

2 If a solid has dissolved in water, how is it able to pass through a filter?

Science Chatterbox 3

SEPARATE

6 Which physical changes occur when a material evaporates?

5 What happens when a material condensates?

filtration (using a filter)

it changes from the **gas state** to the **liquid state**

the **particles** are **much smaller** than the **microscopic holes** of the filter paper - and easily pass through

it changes from the **liquid state** to the **gas state**

a solid which will not dissolve in water (flour chalk, etc)

because it has broken down into particles so small, they can't be seen with the naked eye

© Chris Jones 2008

No, because the blue colour comes from a soluble solid that doesn't evaporate

heat the water - or use more water - or stir it faster

How could you make a soluble solid dissolve faster in water?

7

What does 'insoluble in water' mean?

8

NET

Why can't you see a solid which has dissolved?

4

Carrie boils a solution of water and blue ink, will the steam turn blue?

3

COLANDER

© Chris Jones 2008

Unit 6C

More About Dissolving

Chatterbox 4   Level 4

SOLUBLE

Unit 6C More About Dissolving

1 What effect does the **amount** of **water** have, on the **rate** that a <u>solid dissolves?</u>

2 Same amount of <u>stirs</u>, sugar and water - but different temperatures. What is being investigated?

DISSOLVE

Science Chatterbox 4

5 What is an <u>insoluble</u> <u>substance?</u>

the <u>larger</u> the <u>volume</u> of water, the **faster** the rate a solid dissolves

How does the <u>temperature</u> **affect the rate** that sugar dissolves?

6 What is a **solute?**

a solid that **does not dissolve** in water

a material which **can be dissolved** (e.g. salt, sugar)

a **liquid** which is <u>able to dissolve</u> a <u>soluble</u> <u>solid</u>

washing up liquid orange squash honey

What is a **solvent?**

© Chris Jones 2008

liquid containing a **soluble** <u>solid</u> which has <u>completely</u> <u>dissolved</u>

because sand is an insoluble <u>solid</u>, it <u>stays in the filter</u>, while the <u>water passes through</u>

Give **three** <u>examples</u> of liquids that <u>dissolve in</u> <u>water</u>

7

SOLUTION

4 What is a **solution?**

Why can sand be **separated** from water using the <u>filtration</u> **method?** **3**

EVAPORATE

© Chris Jones 2008

Unit 6C

More About Dissolving

Chatterbox 5   Level 5

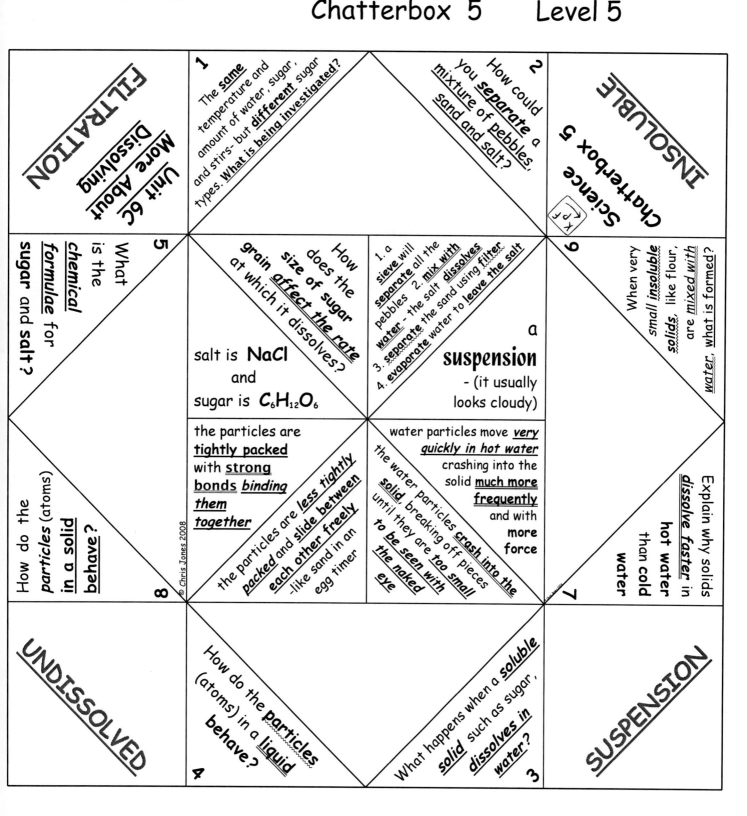

FILTRATION

More About Dissolving

Unit 6C

1 — The **same** temperature and amount of water, sugar, and stirs - but **different** sugar types. **What is being investigated?**

2 — How could you **separate** a mixture of pebbles, sand and salt?

Science Chatterbox 5

INSOLUBLE

5 — What is the **chemical formulae** for **sugar** and **salt**?

How does the **size of sugar grain affect the rate** at which it dissolves?

salt is **NaCl**
and
sugar is $C_6H_{12}O_6$

1.a **sieve** will **separate** all the pebbles 2. **mix with water** - the salt **dissolves** 3. **separate** the sand using **filter** 4. **evaporate** water to **leave the salt**

a **suspension**
- (it usually looks cloudy)

6 — When very small **insoluble solids,** like flour, are **mixed with water,** what is formed?

How do the **particles** (atoms) **in a solid behave?**

the particles are **tightly packed** with **strong bonds** *binding them together*

© Chris Jones 2008

the particles are *less tightly packed* and *slide between each other freely* -like sand in an egg timer

water particles move *very quickly in hot water* crashing into the solid **much more frequently** and with **more force**

the water particles **crash into the** *solid,* breaking off pieces until they are **too small to be seen with the naked eye**

Explain why solids *dissolve faster* in **hot water** than **cold water**

8 —

UNDISSOLVED

How do the **particles** (atoms) in a **liquid** behave?

What happens when a *soluble* **solid** such as sugar, *solid* *dissolves in water?*

SUSPENSION

7 —

3 —

4 —

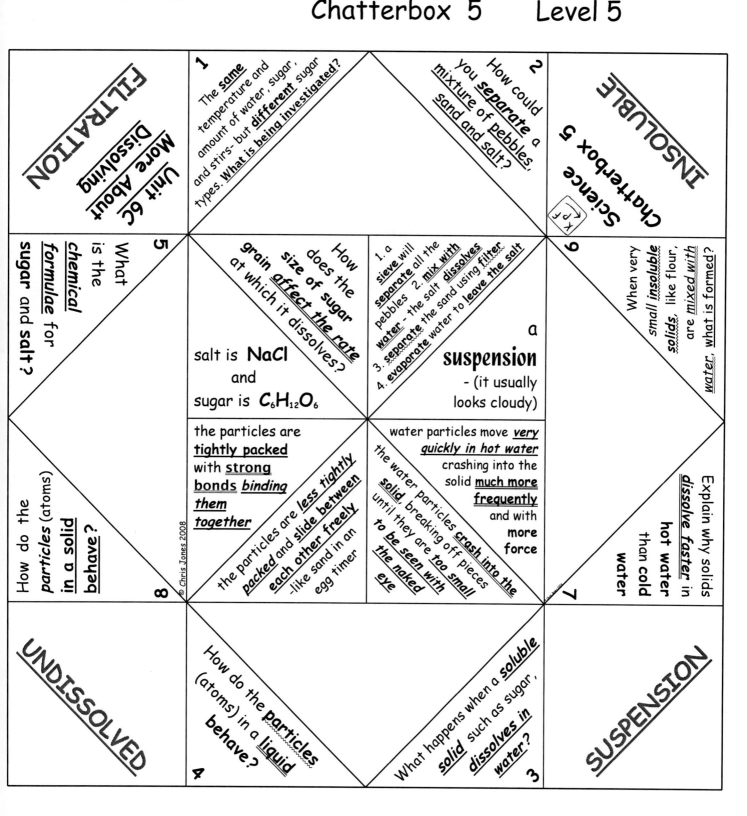

© Chris Jones 2008

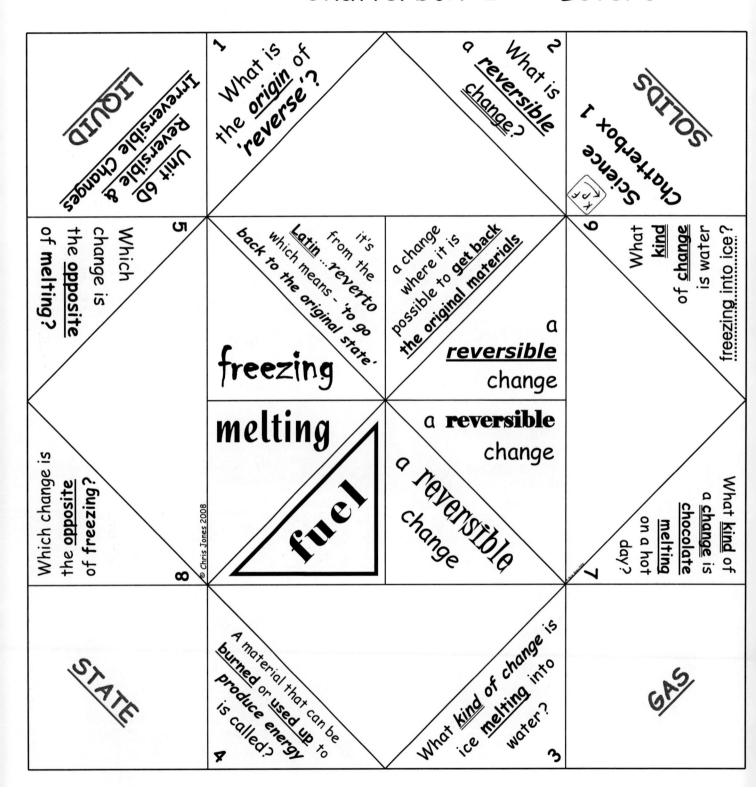

LIQUID

Unit 6D
Reversible &
Irreversible Changes

1 What is the *origin* of the word 'reverse'?

2 What is a *reversible* change?

Science Chatterbox 1

SOLIDS

5 Which change is the *opposite* of melting?

it's from the *Latin* ...reverto which means - 'to go back to the original state'

freezing

melting

fuel

a change where it is possible to *get back* the original materials

a *reversible* change

a **reversible** change

a reversible change

6 What *kind* of *change* is water freezing into ice?

Which change is the *opposite* of freezing?

8

© Chris Jones 2008

7 What *kind* of a *change* is *chocolate* *melting* on a hot day?

STATE

4 A material that can be *burned* or *used up* to produce energy is called?

3 What *kind* of change is ice *melting* into water?

GAS

© Chris Jones 2008

Unit 6D Reversible and Irreversible Changes

Chatterbox 2   Level 3

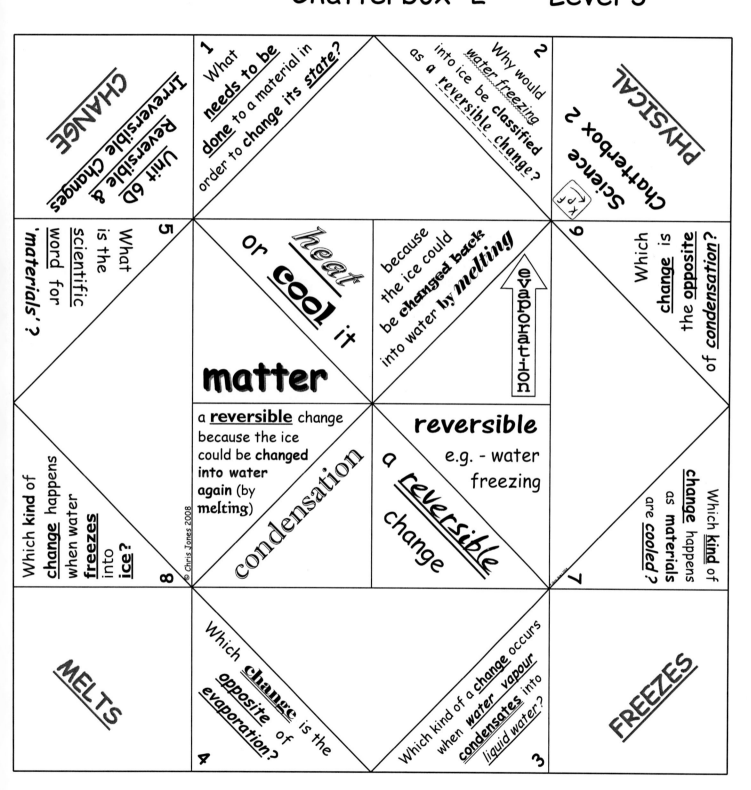

CHANGE

Irreversible

Reversible Changes

Unit 6D

Reversible &

1 What needs to be done to a material in order to change its state?

2 Why would water freezing into ice be classified as a reversible change?

Science Chatterbox 2

PHYSICAL

5 What is the scientific word for 'materials'?

heat or cool it

matter

a **reversible** change because the ice could be **changed into water again** (by melting)

because the ice could be **changed back** into water by **melting**

evaporation

6 Which change is the **opposite** of **condensation**?

Which kind of change happens when water **freezes** into **ice**?

© Chris Jones 2008

condensation

a reversible change

reversible e.g. - water freezing

Which kind of **change** happens as materials are **cooled**?

MELTS

Which **change** is the **opposite** of **evaporation**?

4

Which kind of a **change** occurs when **water vapour condensates** into **liquid water**?

3

FREEZES

7

8

Unit 6D Reversible and Irreversible Changes

Chatterbox 3   Level 3

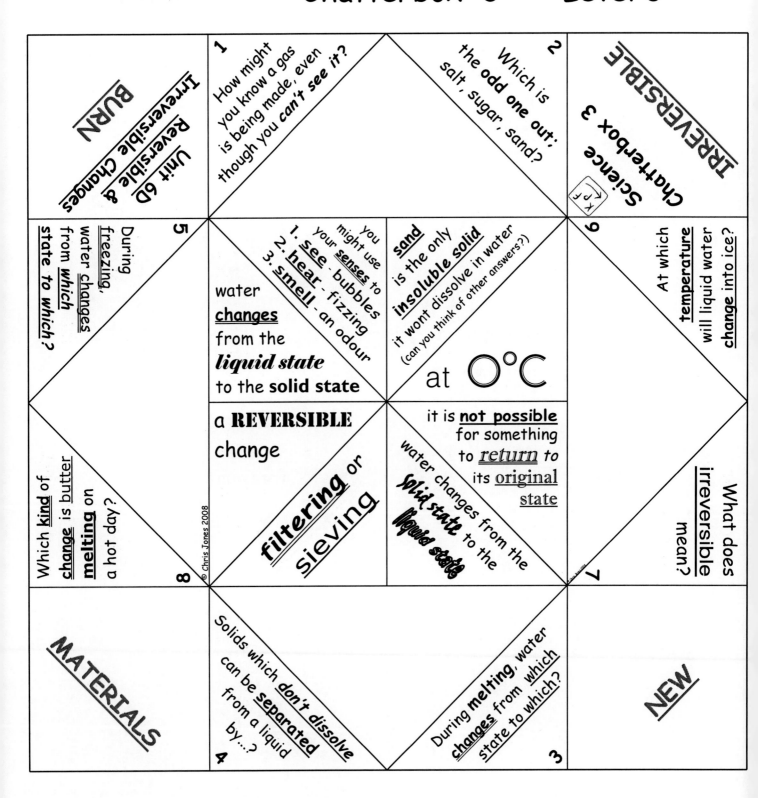

BURN

Irreversible Changes

Reversible &

Unit 6D

1 How might you know a gas is being made, even though you *can't see it?*

2 Which is the odd one out: salt, sugar, sand?

IRREVERSIBLE

Chatterbox 3

Science

5 During *freezing*, water *changes* from *which* state *to which?*

you might use your **senses** to
1. **see** - bubbles
2. **hear** - fizzing
3. **smell** - an odour

water **changes** from the *liquid state* to the **solid state**

sand is the only **insoluble solid** it wont dissolve in water (can you think of other answers?)

6 At which **temperature** will liquid water **change** into ice?

at O°C

a **REVERSIBLE** change

it is **not possible** for something to *return* to its **original** **state**

Which **kind** of **change** is butter **melting** on a hot day?

© Chris Jones 2008

filtering or *sieving*

water changes from the *solid state* to the *liquid state*

What does **irreversible** mean?

8

7

MATERIALS

Solids which *don't dissolve* can be **separated** from a liquid by...?

During **melting**, water **changes** from *which* state to *which?*

NEW

4

3

© Chris Jones 2008

Unit 6D — Reversible and Irreversible Changes

Chatterbox 4   Level 4

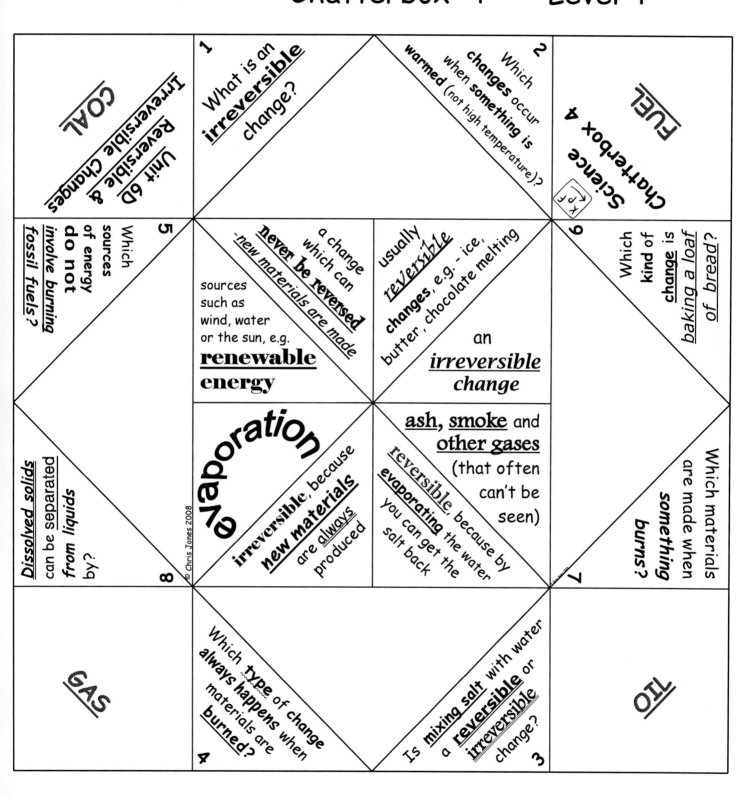

Unit 6D
Reversible &
Irreversible Changes
COAL

1 What is an **irreversible change?**

2 Which **changes** occur when **something** is **warmed** (not high temperature)?

Science Chatterbox 4
FUEL

5 Which sources of energy **do not** involve burning fossil fuels?

a change which can **never be reversed** - new materials are made

sources such as wind, water or the sun, e.g. **renewable energy**

usually **reversible** changes, e.g. - ice, butter, chocolate melting

an **irreversible change**

6 Which kind of change is baking a loaf of bread?

evaporation

irreversible, because **new materials** **are always** produced

reversible, because by **evaporating** the water you can get the salt back

ash, smoke and **other gases** (that often can't be seen)

8 *Dissolved solids* can be separated *from liquids* by?

© Chris Jones 2008

7 Which materials are made when **something burns?**

OIL

GAS

4 Which **type** of change always happens when materials are **burned?**

3 Is **mixing salt** with water a **reversible** or **irreversible** change?

Unit 6D — Reversible and Irreversible Changes

Chatterbox 5   Level 4

REVERSIBLE

Irreversible &
Reversible Changes

Unit 6D

1 When materials are burned - as well as smoke and ash - which <u>two</u> forms of energy are produced?

2 Why is baking bread classified as an <u>irreversible change</u>?

EVAPORATE

Science Chatterbox 5

6 Why are <u>irreversible</u> changes .... irreversible?

5 Coal, oil and gas are examples of which <u>fuel type</u>?

heat and **light**

fossil **fuel**

a new product has been made, you <u>can't get back</u> the flour, yeast and water

because <u>new materials</u> have been made

an <u>irreversible</u> change

What <u>kind</u> of a <u>change</u> is frying an egg?

Which is the <u>odd one out</u>: lemon juice, water vinegar?

<s>water</s>, because the <u>others are acids</u>

(can you think of other answers)

© Chris Jones 2008

<u>irreversible</u>, because the chalk fizzes -and <u>new materials are made</u> (the gas is CO_2)

water <u>changes</u> from the <u>gas</u> state to the <u>liquid</u> state

8

7

CONDENSATE

Is mixing vinegar and chalk a <u>reversible</u> or <u>irreversible</u> change?

4

During <u>condensation</u>, water changes from which state to which?

3

MELTING

© Chris Jones 2008

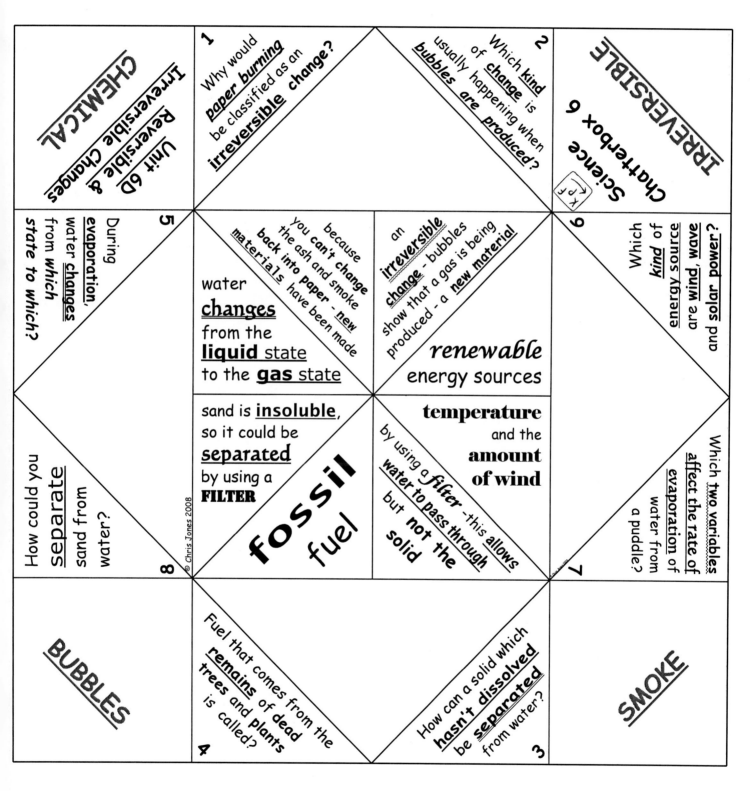

CHEMICAL

Irreversible &
Reversible Changes

Unit 6D

1
Why would *paper burning* be classified as an *irreversible* change?

2
Which *kind* of *change* is usually happening when *bubbles are produced?*

IRREVERSIBLE

Science
Chatterbox 6

5
During *evaporation*, water *changes* from *which* *state to which?*

because you *can't change* the ash and smoke *back into paper* - *new materials* have been made

an *irreversible change* - bubbles show that a gas is being produced - a *new material*

6
Which *kind* of *energy source* are *wind, wave* and *solar power?*

water *changes* from the **liquid** state to the **gas** state

renewable energy sources

sand is **insoluble**, so it could be **separated** by using a **FILTER**

temperature and the **amount of wind**

by using a *filter* - this allows *water to pass through* but **not the** solid

Which *two variables* *affect the rate of* *evaporation* of water from a puddle?

How could you *separate* sand from water?

© Chris Jones 2008

fossil fuel

8

7

How can a solid which *hasn't dissolved* be *separated* from water?

SMOKE

BUBBLES

Fuel that comes from the *remains* of dead *trees and plants* is called?

4

3

Unit 6D — Reversible and Irreversible Changes

Chatterbox 7   Level 5

INSOLUBLE

Irreversible &
Reversible Changes
Unit 6D

1 Describe the *changes* as a candle is burned

2 What is the **evidence** that mixing cement and water is an **irreversible change**?

FILTRATION

Science
Chatterbox 7

5 Which scientific **enquiry skill** is usually used to **identify irreversible changes**?

1. wax **melts** from solid to liquid
2. liquid **evaporates** into gas
3. gas **burns** making **new materials**

the mixture heats up, then turns rock hard as it dries - it's **changed into** a new material

concrete = a new material

chemical changes

6 **Irreversible** changes, where **new materials** are **made**, are also called?

observation such as smoke from burning paper

the **larger** the jar the **longer** a candle will burn

© Chris Jones 2008

ALL the **oxygen** is used up as it **burns**, (**carbon dioxide** (CO_2) is released)

because there is **more oxygen**, so the candle **burns for longer**

bubbles are produced, which proves that **new materials** are being made

Explain why a candle **burns longer** in a **larger jar**

7

What **effect** does the **jar size** have on the **time a candle burns?**

8

SIEVES

4 Why does a candle burning in a jar, **eventually go out?**

What is the **evidence** that mixing lemon juice and bicarbonate of soda is an **example** of an **irreversible change?**

3

RENEWABLE

82

© Chris Jones 2008

Unit 6E   Balanced and Unbalanced Forces

Chatterbox 1   Level 3

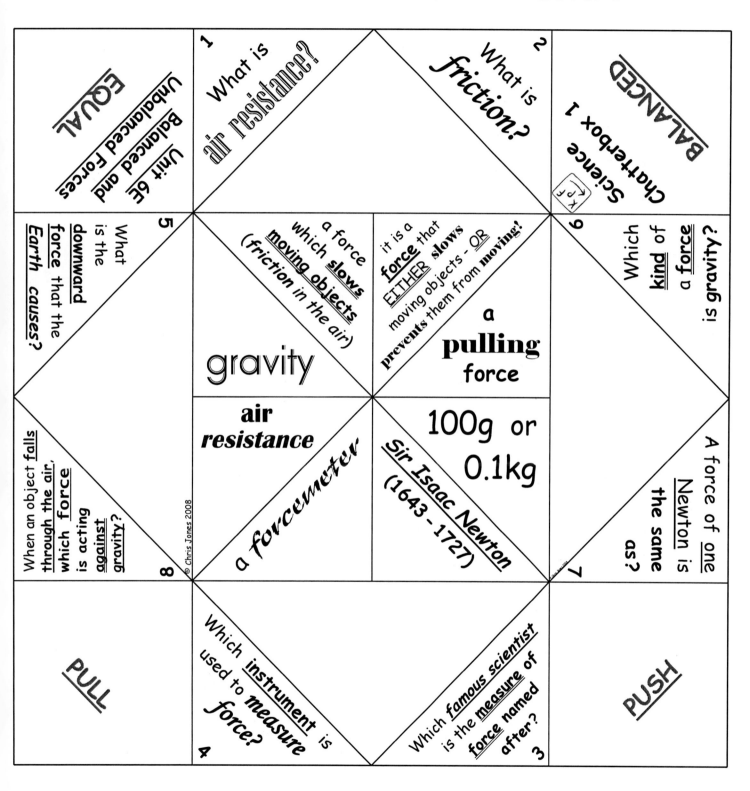

EQUAL

Unit 6E
Balanced and Unbalanced Forces

1 What is air resistance?

2 What is friction?

Science Chatterbox 1

BALANCED

5 What is the downward force that the Earth causes?

a force which slows moving objects (friction in the air)

it is a force that EITHER slows moving objects - OR prevents them from moving!

a pulling force

6 Which kind of a force is gravity?

gravity

air resistance

a forcemeter

Sir Isaac Newton (1643 - 1727)

100g or 0.1kg

When an object falls through the air, which force is acting against gravity?

8

© Chris Jones 2008

A force of one Newton is the same as?

7

PULL

4 Which instrument is used to measure force?

3 Which famous scientist is the measure of force named after?

PUSH

© Chris Jones 2008

WEIGHT

Unit 6E
Balanced and
Unbalanced Forces

1
What is friction called, if air is one of the surfaces?

2
The Newton is used to measure what?

GRAVITY

Science Chatterbox 2

What is friction called when water is one of the surfaces?

5
When a parachute falls, which two forces are acting on it?

air resistance

gravity and **air resistance**

upthrust

a spring

1. **force,**
2. **weight,** or
3. **pull of gravity,**
(they are all related!)

water resistance

1600g or **1.6kg**

because of the pull of *gravity*

What is friction called when water is one of the surfaces?

A force of 16 Newtons is the same as?

© Chris Jones 2008

The force, caused by water, which pushes up, is called?

8

FORCEMETER

4
What is the important moving part inside a forcemeter?

Why do objects fall towards the Earth?

3

MEASURE

7

© Chris Jones 2008

Unit 6E   Balanced and Unbalanced Forces

Chatterbox 3   Level 4

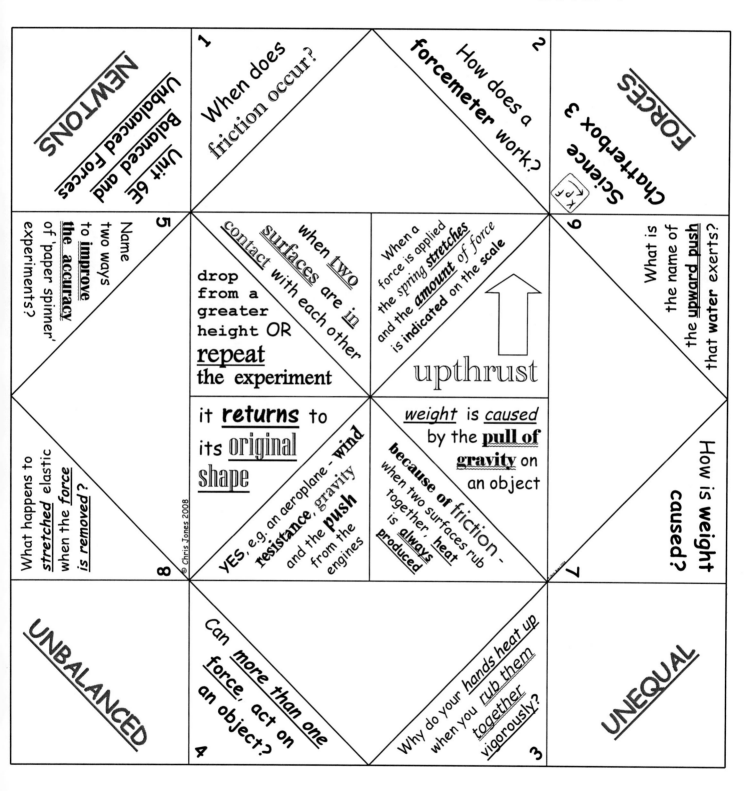

NEWTONS
Unbalanced
Balanced Forces
Unit 6E

1 When does friction occur?

2 How does a forcemeter work?

FORCES
Science Chatterbox 3

5 Name two ways to **improve the accuracy** of 'paper spinner' experiments?

when **two** surfaces are **in contact** with each other

drop from a greater height OR **repeat** the experiment

When a force is applied the spring **stretches** and the **amount** of force is indicated on the scale

upthrust

6 What is the name of the **upward push** that **water exerts**?

What happens to **stretched** elastic when the **force is removed**?

it **returns** to its original shape

YES, e.g. an aeroplane – **wind resistance**, gravity and the **push** from the engines

because of friction – when two surfaces rub together, heat is **always produced**

weight is **caused** by the **pull of gravity** on an object

How is **weight caused**?

© Chris Jones 2008

UNBALANCED

4 Can **more than one force** act on an object?

3 Why do your **hands heat up** when you **rub them together** vigorously?

UNEQUAL

© Chris Jones 2008

Unit 6E   Balanced and Unbalanced Forces

Chatterbox 4   Level 4

Unit 6E Balanced and Unbalanced Forces

REDUCE

1 How does the **number of** paperclips on a spinner **affect the speed it falls?**

2 Explain why an object **weighs less** in **water** than in **air**

Science Chatterbox 4

FRICTION

5 Which symbol is used to show the **direction a force is acting?**

the **more** paperclips, the **faster** it falls

an **arrow**

because the 'upward push' of the water's upthrust, **cancels out** some of the 'pulling down' of gravity

they are streamlined to **reduce air resistance**

6 Why are rockets and planes **pointed at one end?**

8 What **effect** does the **size** of a parachute have on the **rate it descends?**

the **larger** the parachute, the **slower** it descends

© Chris Jones 2008

they must be **dropped** from the **same height**

the forces of **gravity** and **upthrust** are **balanced**

because of the **Moon's gravity** - it pulls the Earth's water towards it

7 Why do we have **tides?**

STREAMLINED

4 Two identical pieces of paper, one flat and **one screwed up**, are **dropped simultaneously**. What else is needed to make this a fair test?

3 What is **happening** when a boat is **floating?**

LUBRICATE

86

© Chris Jones 2008

Unit 6E

Balanced and Unbalanced Forces

Chatterbox 5   Level 4

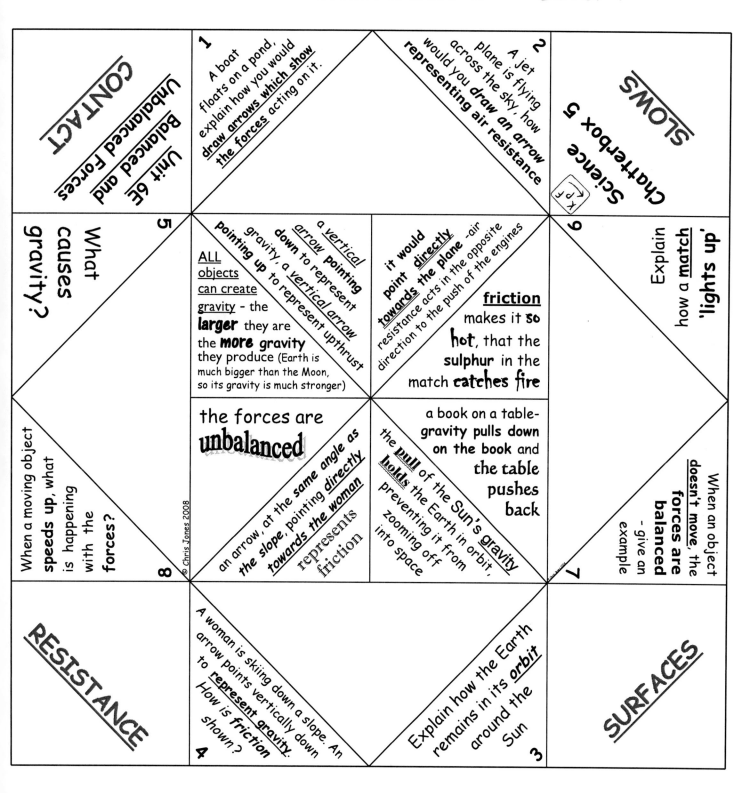

CONTACT

Unit 6E Balanced and Unbalanced Forces

1 A boat floats on a pond, explain how you would <u>draw arrows</u> <u>which show</u> <u>the forces</u> acting on it.

2 A jet plane is flying across the sky, how would you **draw an arrow** **representing air resistance**

SLOWS

Science Chatterbox 5

5 What causes gravity?

<u>a vertical</u> <u>arrow</u> **pointing** **down** to represent gravity, a vertical arrow **pointing up** to represent upthrust

<u>ALL</u> <u>objects</u> <u>can create</u> gravity - the **larger** they are the **more** gravity they produce (Earth is much bigger than the Moon, so its gravity is much stronger)

it would **point** <u>directly</u> <u>towards the plane</u> -air resistance acts in the opposite direction to the push of the engines

friction makes it **so** **hot**, that the **sulphur** in the match **catches fire**

6 Explain how a <u>match</u> 'lights up'.

When an object <u>doesn't move</u>, the **forces are** **balanced** - give an example

the forces are **unbalanced**

an arrow, at the same angle as the slope, pointing <u>directly</u> <u>towards the woman</u> represents friction

a book on a table- gravity pulls down **on the book** and **the table** **pushes** **back**

<u>the **pull** of the Sun's **gravity**</u> **holds** the Earth in orbit, preventing it from zooming off into space

7

When a moving object **speeds up**, what is happening with the **forces**?

8 © Chris Jones 2008

SURFACES

RESISTANCE

4 A woman is skiing down a slope. An arrow points vertically down to **represent gravity.** How is **friction** shown?

3 Explain how the Earth remains in its <u>orbit</u> around the Sun

© Chris Jones 2008

Unit 6E   Balanced and Unbalanced Forces

Chatterbox 6   Level 5

UPTHRUST

Unbalanced and Balanced Forces

Unit 6E

1 A helium balloon with 8 paperclips, _stays floating_ in _mid - air_. How would the forces acting on it **be represented?**

2 A woman is skiing down a slope. How would you draw the arrows _representing the_ _forces of friction and gravity?_

Science Chatterbox 6

WATER

5 Which **4 forces** are acting on a boat which is _steadily travelling in a straight line?_

an _arrow pointing down_ for **gravity**, and _one_ _arrow_ _pointing up_ for the **upward** **push** of the helium. They will be _the same size_ - because they are **balanced**

1. **pull of gravity** 2. **push of upthrust** (from the water) 3. **push of the propeller** 4. **water resistance** against the boat (**friction**)

a vertical arrow pointing down- GRAVITY. _An_ _arrow, at the same angle_ _as the slope, pointing directly_ _towards the woman_ - FRICTION

the **higher** the spinner, the **longer** it takes to fall

6 How does the _height,_ from which a spinner is dropped, _affect the time it_ _takes to fall?_

8 A spinner with **4** paperclips **falls** **faster** than one with **2** - paperclips Why?

© Chris Jones 2008

more paperclips will **increase** the **weight** but **not** the _air resistance_ -so it falls **FASTER**

the two forces are **not balanced**- it falls to earth because the pull of **gravity** is much **stronger** than **air resistance**

the _heavier the_ _weight_, the **more** an elastic band **stretches**

A **small** arrow pointing down for **gravity**, and a **large** arrow _pointing up_ for the _'upward push'_ of the balloon

7 What effect does _increasing the_ _weight_ of an object, have on elastic bands?

WEIGHT

REDUCED

4 Two forces, **air resistance** and **gravity**, act on a parachute. Explain **why** it will always _fall to the ground_

3 A helium balloon floats upwards until it is out of sight. How would you **represent** _the forces acting_ on it?

© Chris Jones 2008

Unit 6E   Balanced and Unbalanced Forces

Chatterbox 7   Level 5

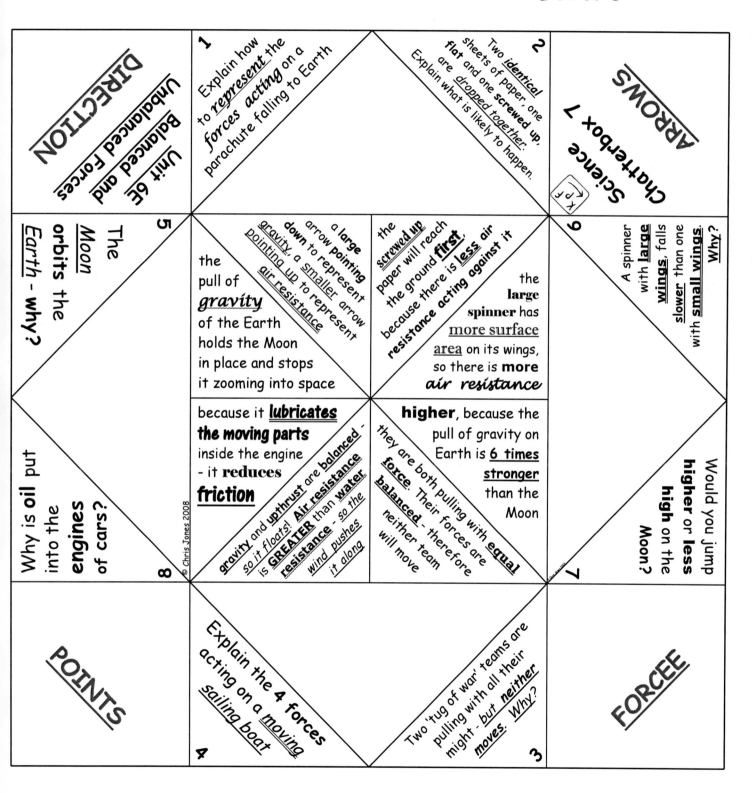

DIRECTION

Unit 6E Balanced and Unbalanced Forces

1 Explain how to *represent* the *forces acting* on a parachute falling to Earth

2 Two *identical* sheets of paper, one *flat* and one *screwed up*, are *dropped together*. Explain what is likely to happen.

Science Chatterbox 7

ARROWS

5 The *Moon* *orbits* the *Earth - why?*

the pull of *gravity* of the Earth holds the Moon in place and stops it zooming into space

a **large** arrow pointing **down** to represent *gravity*, a **smaller** arrow pointing **up** to represent *air resistance*

the *screwed up* paper will reach the ground **first** because there is *less air resistance acting against it*

the **large spinner** has *more surface area* on its wings, so there is **more** *air resistance*

6 A spinner with **large wings**, falls **slower** than one with **small wings**. **Why?**

Why is **oil** put into the **engines of cars?**

because it **lubricates the moving parts** inside the engine - it **reduces friction**

gravity and **upthrust** are balanced - *so it floats!* *Air resistance* is **GREATER** than **water** *resistance - so the wind pushes it along*

they are both pulling with **equal** *force*. Their forces are *balanced* - therefore neither team will move

higher, because the pull of gravity on Earth is **6 times stronger** than the Moon

Would you jump **higher or less high** on the **Moon?**

POINTS

4 Explain the 4 forces acting on a *moving* *sailing boat*

3 Two 'tug of war' teams are pulling with all their might - *but **neither** moves. Why?*

FORCEE

© Chris Jones 2008

MATERIAL

Unit 6F How We See Things

1 Which kind of surfaces are **shiny**?

How is a **shadow formed**? 2

OPAQUE

Science Chatterbox 1

5 Why do some objects seem **shiny**?

usually **smooth & hard** surfaces, because they are better at reflecting light

because they can **reflect more light** than surrounding objects

when light, from a light source, is blocked by an opaque object

the absence of light

6 What is **darkness**?

the sun

light is a <u>form of energy</u> which we can detect with our eyes

anything that **produces light**, e.g. the Sun

the <u>torch</u>, because it is the <u>only source of light</u>

What is meant by a **primary light source**?

© Chris Jones 2008

Where does **daylight** come from? 8

TRANSLUCENT

What is **light**? 4

Which is the **odd one out**: mirror, Moon, torch, yellow flower, window? 3

TRANSPARENT 7

© Chris Jones 2008

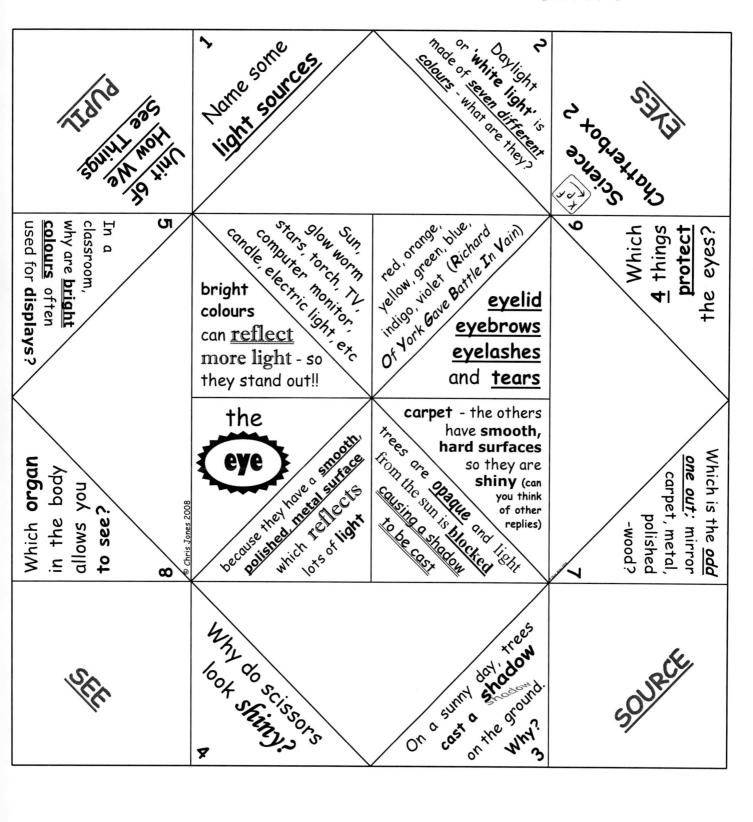

1. Name some **light sources**

2. Daylight or '**white light**' is made of **seven different colours** - what are they?

Science Chatterbox 2 **EYES**

Which **4 things protect the eyes?**

PUPIL
How We See Things
Unit 6F

5. In a classroom, why are **bright colours** often used for **displays?**

bright colours can **reflect** more light - so they stand out!!

Sun, glow worm stars, torch, TV, computer monitor, candle, electric light, etc

red, orange, yellow, green, blue, indigo, violet (*Richard Of York Gave Battle In Vain*)

eyelid eyebrows eyelashes and **tears**

Which is the **odd one out**: mirror carpet, metal, polished -wood?

the **eye**

© Chris Jones 2008

because they have a **smooth, polished, metal surface** which **reflects** lots of **light**

carpet - the others have **smooth, hard surfaces** so they are **shiny** (can you think of other replies)

trees are **opaque** and light from the sun is **blocked causing a shadow to be cast**

Which **organ** in the body allows you **to see?**

8.

SEE

4. Why do scissors look **shiny?**

3. On a sunny day, trees **cast a** shadow **shadow** on the ground. **Why?**

7. SOURCE

© Chris Jones 2008

LIGHT

How We See Things

Unit 6F

1 What is a **translucent** material?

2 How are we able to **see objects?**

Science Chatterbox 3

TRAVELS

5 What happens to a shadow as the Sun **appears** to move across the sky?

a material which **allows some, but not all,** of the light to pass through

the **position** and **size** changes

we see objects when light is reflected off them and travels **directly into our eyes**

a material which **doesn't allow ANY** light to **pass through**

6 What is an **opaque** material?

its **direction of travel changes**

1. move the light closer to the object OR 2. move the object closer to the light

a **transparent** material

because they **don't reflect much light** - most of it is **absorbed**

Why do dark materials look **dark?**

© Chris Jones 2008

8 What happens when a beam of light **reflects** from a surface?

7

LINE

4 Give two ways you could make a **shadow larger**

Which name is given to a material which *allows all the light to pass through?*

3

STRAIGHT

© Chris Jones 2008

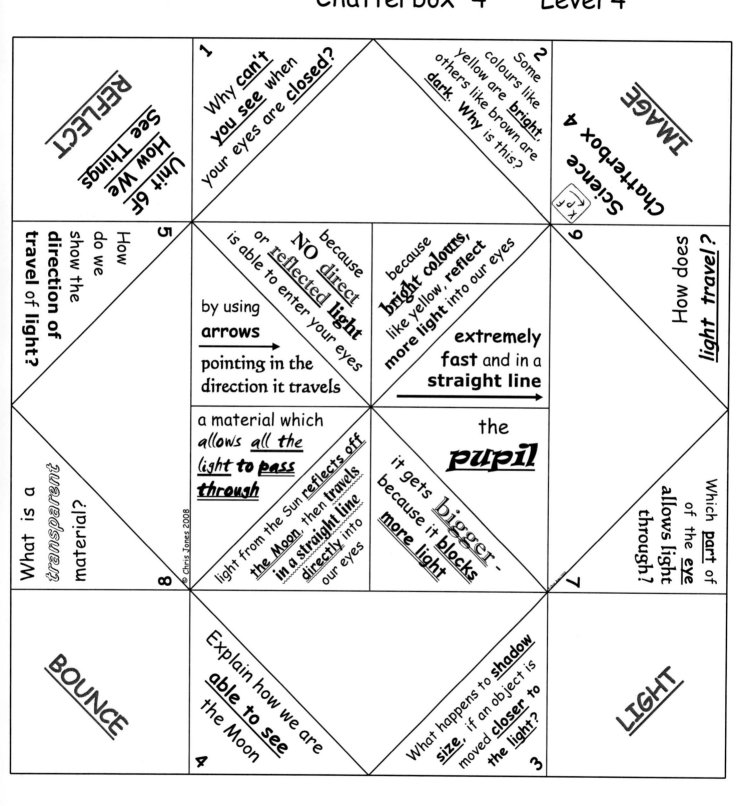

REFLECT

How We See Things

Unit 6F

1
Why can't you see when your eyes are closed?

2
Some colours like yellow are bright, others like brown are dark. Why is this?

Science Chatterbox 4

IMAGE

5
How do we show the direction of travel of light?

because NO direct or reflected light is able to enter your eyes

by using arrows pointing in the direction it travels

because bright colours, like yellow, reflect more light into our eyes

extremely fast and in a straight line

6
How does light travel?

What is a transparent material?

a material which allows all the light to pass through

© Chris Jones 2008

light from the Sun reflects off the Moon, then travels in a straight line directly into our eyes

it gets bigger - because it blocks more light

the pupil

Which part of the eye allows light through?

8

7

BOUNCE

Explain how we are able to see the Moon

4

What happens to shadow size, if an object is moved closer to the light?

3

LIGHT

© Chris Jones 2008

Unit 6F

How We See Things

Chatterbox 5   Level 4

BRIGHT

Unit 6F How We See Things

1 How do we know that light **travels** in **straight lines?**

2 Why do so many cyclists wear **reflective clothes** at night?

SHINY

Science Chatterbox 5

5 How could you get light to travel **around a corner?**

because **shadows are formed** - if it could bend around objects, there wouldn't be **any shadows**

because **light** from car headlights **reflects back** into the drivers eyes - so the cyclist can be seen!

6 Which kind of surface **doesn't reflect any light at all?**

the only way would be to **reflect** it off something, - like a mirror

a **matt-black** surface

How does the eye **control how much** light enters?

light enters through the pupil - which is LARGE or SMALL depending on **how bright** the light is

© Chris Jones 2008

because the Sun is at **different positions**, so the angle of the sunlight **changes through the day**

at **sunrise** and **sunset**, because the Sun is **very** low **in the sky**

they **reflect more light** and **stand out** to **attract** bees and other **insects**

Which time of day are shadows **longest** in length?

8

7

REFLECTIVE

Why does shadow length **change** during the day?

Why are flower petals usually **bright colours?**

MIRRORS

4

3

94

© Chris Jones 2008

Unit 6F

How We See Things

Chatterbox 6   Level 5

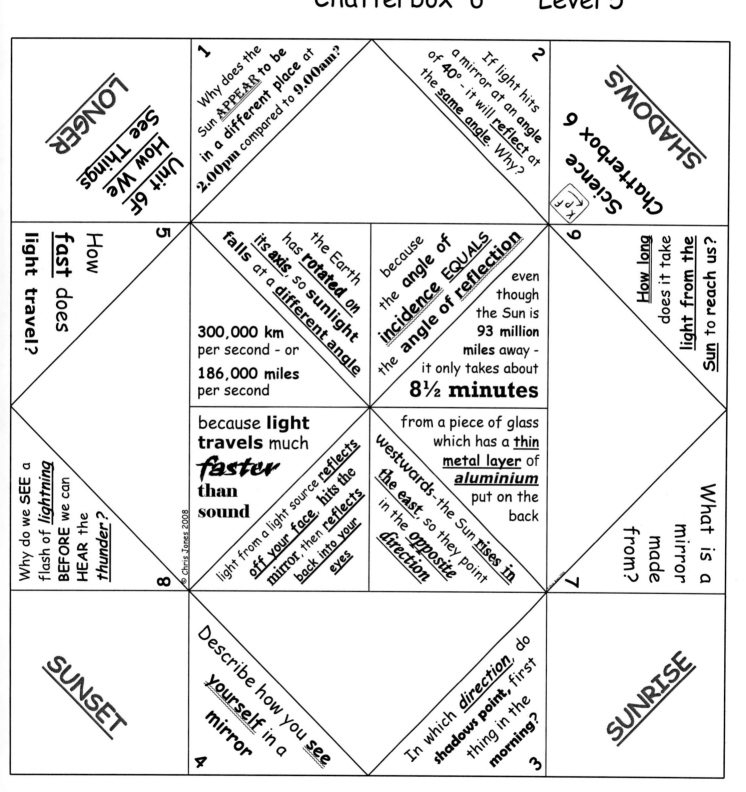

1 Why does the Sun <u>APPEAR</u> to be in a different place at 2.00pm compared to **9.00am?**

2 If light hits a mirror at an angle of 40° - it will <u>reflect</u> at the <u>same angle</u>. Why?

SHADOWS

Science Chatterbox 6

LONGER

Unit 6F How We See Things

5 How <u>fast</u> does **light travel?**

the Earth has **rotated** on its <u>axis</u>, so <u>sunlight</u> falls at a **different angle**

300,000 km per second - or 186,000 miles per second

because the **angle of** <u>incidence</u> **EQUALS** the **angle of reflection**

even though the Sun is 93 million miles away - it only takes about **8½ minutes**

How long does it take <u>light from the</u> <u>Sun</u> to reach us?

6

because **light travels** much *faster* **than sound**

light from a light source <u>reflects</u> <u>off your face</u>, hits the <u>mirror</u>, then <u>reflects</u> <u>back into your eyes</u>

<u>westwards</u>-the Sun <u>rises in</u> <u>the east</u>, so they point in the **opposite direction**

from a piece of glass which has a <u>thin</u> <u>metal layer</u> of <u>aluminium</u> put on the back

What is a mirror made from?

7

8 Why do we SEE a flash of <u>lightning</u> **BEFORE** we can **HEAR** the <u>thunder?</u>

© Chris Jones 2008

4 Describe how you <u>see</u> **yourself** in a **mirror**

3 In which <u>direction</u> do <u>shadows point</u> first thing in the **morning?**

SUNSET

SUNRISE

© Chris Jones 2008

Unit 6G

Changing Circuits

Chatterbox 1   Level 3

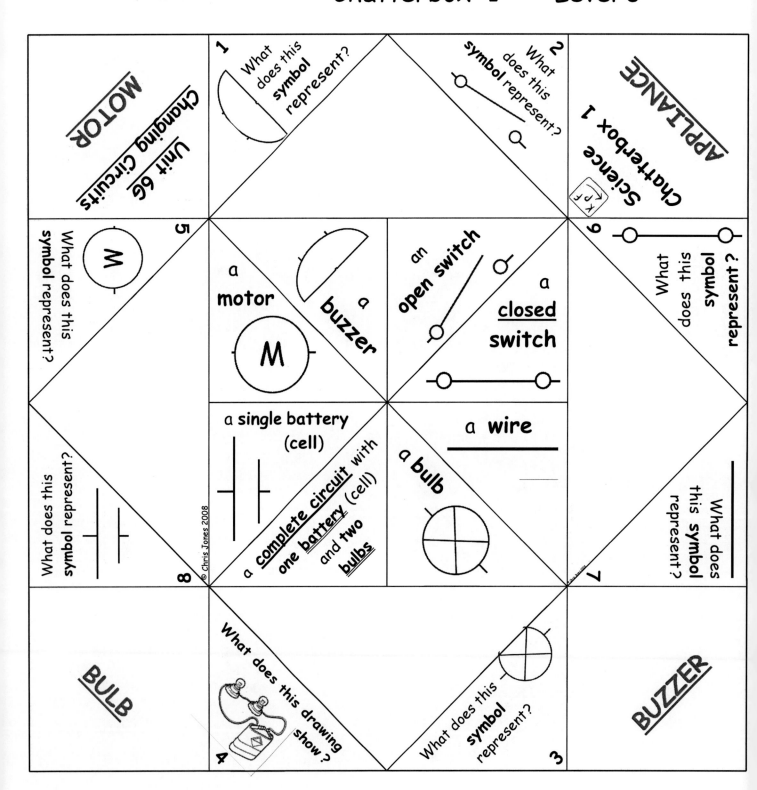

MOTOR

Changing Circuits

Unit 6G

Science Chatterbox 1

APPLIANCE

1 What does this **symbol** represent?

2 What does this **symbol** represent?

5 What does this symbol represent?

a **motor**

M

a **buzzer**

an **open switch**

a **closed switch**

6 What does this **symbol** represent?

© Chris Jones 2008

a single battery (cell)

a complete circuit with one battery (cell) and two bulbs

a **wire**

a **bulb**

What does this **symbol** represent?

What does this symbol represent?

BULB

What does this drawing show?

4

What does this **symbol** represent?

3

BUZZER

W

M

© Chris Jones 2008

Unit 6G

Changing Circuits

Chatterbox 2   Level 3

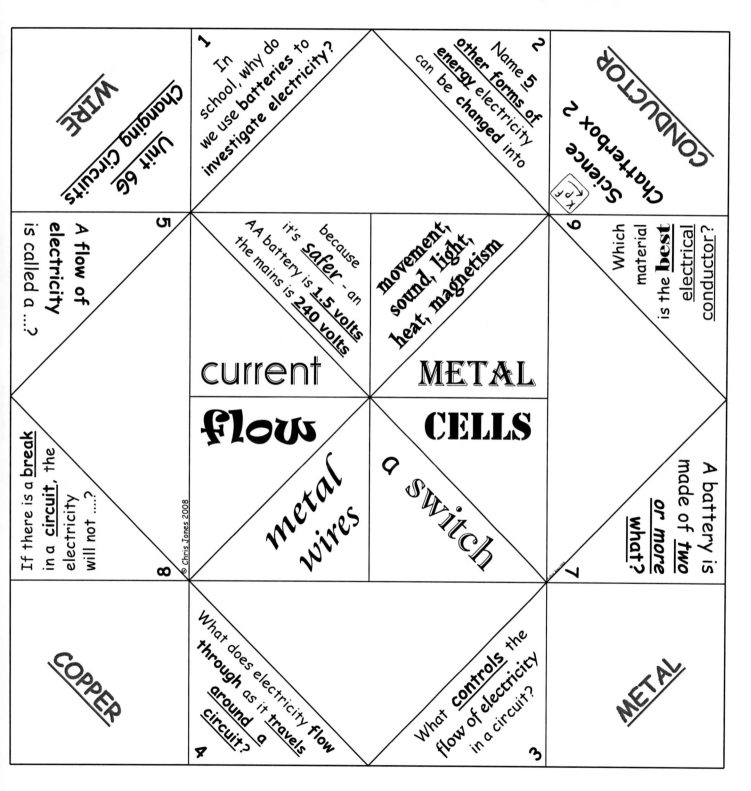

WIRE

Changing Circuits

Unit 6G

1 In school, why do we use batteries to investigate electricity?

2 Name 5 other forms of energy electricity can be changed into

CONDUCTOR

Science Chatterbox 2

5 A flow of electricity is called a ....?

because it's **safer** - an AA battery is **1.5 volts** the mains is **240 volts**

movement, sound, light, heat, magnetism

current

flow

METAL

CELLS

6 Which material is the **best** electrical conductor?

If there is a **break** in a **circuit**, the electricity will not ....?

metal wires

a switch

A battery is made of **two** **or more** **what?**

© Chris Jones 2008

8

7

COPPER

4 What does electricity flow **through** as it **travels** **around** a **circuit?**

What **controls** the flow of electricity in a circuit?

METAL

3

© Chris Jones 2008

Changing Circuits

Chatterbox 3   Level 3

CONTROL

Unit 6G Changing Circuits

1 How is a battery containing three 1.5V cells labelled?

2 What is the **purpose** of a **switch**?

Science Chatterbox 3

SWITCH

5 Which **symbols** do you find on _all batteries?_

4.5V

a **plus** and a **minus** sign (+ and −)

to **control** the **flow of electricity** _around a circuit_

electricity

6 What travels around a _pump_ a _complete circuit?_

ELECTRICAL APPLIANCES

© Chris Jones 2008

because they are very _easy to understand_ and _easy to draw_

positive pole

copper

The end of the battery with the **plus (+) sign** is called the .....?

8 A toaster and kettle are **examples** of what?

OPEN

4 Why are **symbols** used to draw electrical circuits?

Wires are usually made of this **metal** because it is an **excellent** conductor 3

CLOSED

© Chris Jones 2008

Unit 6G

Changing Circuits

Chatterbox 4   Level 3

CELL

Unit 6G changing circuits

1 What is needed for an _electrical appliance_ to work?

2 Name three electrical appliances that _change_ electricity into _light_

Science Chatterbox 4

BATTERY

5 Name **three** electrical appliances that _change_ electricity into _sound_

it must be part of a _complete circuit_ with electricity _flowing through_

vacuum cleaner, radio, TV

torches light bulbs computer monitors

torch
I-Pod
mobile phone

6 Name 3 electrical appliances which use _battery power_

a plug

electric lawn mower, washing machine, electric drill

toaster, hair-drier electric cooker -can you think of others?

electric cooker vacuum cleaner fridge-freezer _can you name more?_

Name 3 electrical appliances that use _mains power_

What goes into a _socket_?

© Chris Jones 2008

8   **7**

POSITIVE

4 Name **three** electrical appliances that _change_ electricity into _movement_

Name three electrical appliances that _change_ electricity into _heat_ **3**

VOLTS

© Chris Jones 2008

Unit 6G

Changing Circuits

Chatterbox 5   Level 4

COMPLETE

Unit 6G
Changing Circuits

1 What is an electrical <u>insulator</u>?

2 Name some appliances which use **dimmer switches**

Science Chatterbox 5

CIRCUIT

a material which <u>doesn't</u> <u>allow</u> electricity to **pass through**

radios, lights, drills, electric cookers, televisions, toasters

What do we call a <u>drawing</u> which uses <u>symbols</u> to <u>represent</u> a circuit?

5 How does a **dimmer switch** work?

it <u>REDUCES</u> the <u>flow</u> of electricity - it is a '<u>*resistor*</u>'

a **circuit diagram**

6

© Chris Jones 2008

a material which <u>allows</u> electricity to <u>**flow through easily**</u>

a material that allows some electricity through, **but not all**

because metal is **an electrical conductor**

<u>li**g**ht</u> and <u>sound</u> energy (plus a small amount of <u>heat</u> energy)

Why are **wires** made from **metal**?

What is an electrical <u>conductor</u>?

8

What is an electrical <u>resistor</u>?

Televisions can **change** electricity into <u>which</u> other kinds of energy?

7

FLOW

ELECTRICITY

4

3

100

© Chris Jones 2008

Unit 6G

Changing Circuits

Chatterbox 6   Level 4

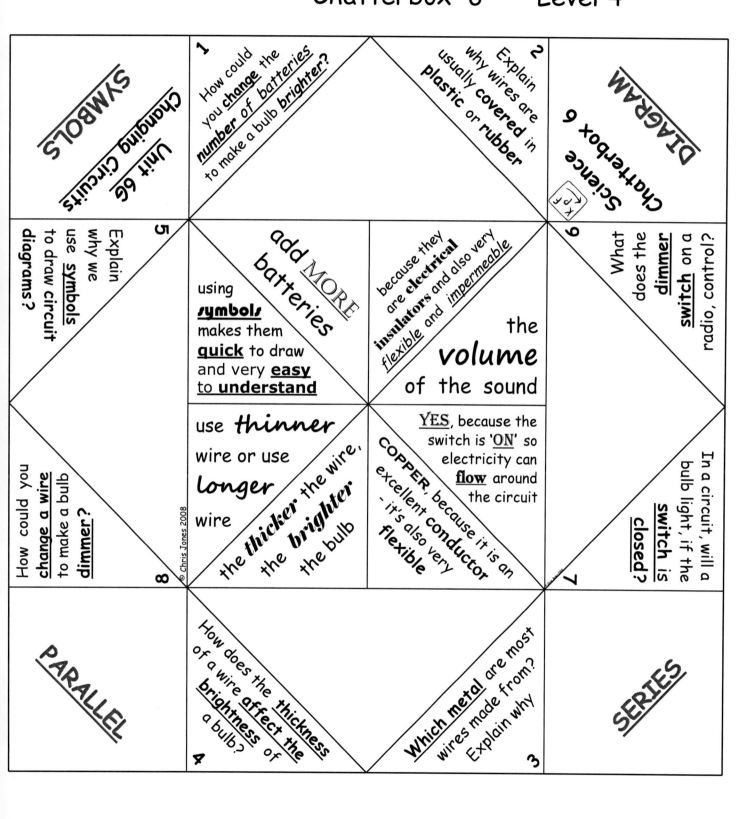

SYMBOLS

Unit 6G Changing Circuits

1 How could you **change** the **number of batteries** to make a bulb **brighter**?

2 Explain why wires are usually **covered** in **plastic** or **rubber**

DIAGRAM

Science Chatterbox 6

5 Explain why we use **symbols** to draw circuit diagrams?

add MORE batteries

using **symbols** makes them **quick** to draw and very **easy** to **understand**

because they are **electrical insulators** and also very **flexible** and **impermeable**

the **volume** of the sound

6 What does the **dimmer switch** on a radio, control?

use **thinner** wire or use **longer** wire

the **thicker** the wire, the **brighter** the bulb

YES, because the switch is '**ON**' so electricity can **flow** around the circuit

COPPER, because it is an excellent **conductor** - it's also very **flexible**

In a circuit, will a bulb light, if the **switch is closed?**

7

© Chris Jones 2008

8 How could you **change a wire** to make a bulb **dimmer?**

PARALLEL

4 How does the **thickness** of a wire **affect the brightness** of a bulb?

3 **Which metal** are most wires made from? Explain why

SERIES

© Chris Jones 2008

BRIGHTER

Changing Circuits

Unit 6G

1 How does the **number of batteries** _affect_ the _brightness_ of a bulb?

2 Give **4 ways** to **reduce** the **brightness** of a bulb

Science Chatterbox 7

BULB

5 How could you **CHANGE** the _number_ of _batteries_ to make a **bulb dimmer?**

the more **batteries**, the **brighter** the bulb (but too many, and it will blow!)

lengthen the wire, use **thinner** wire, add **more bulbs**, **take away a battery**

use **thicker** wire or use SHORTER wire

6 How could you **change** the **wire** to make a bulb **brighter?**

take away batteries

parallel and **series**

add a battery, **shorten** the wire, or use **thicker** wire

longer the the wire, the **dimmer** the bulb

the **larger the number of** **bulbs**, the **dimmer** they will be

How does the **length of a wire** _affect_ how **bright** a bulb is?

© Chris Jones 2008

Name two _types_ of **circuit**

8

7

THICKER

Give **3 ways** to **increase** the **brightness** of a bulb

4

How do the _number of_ _bulbs_ in a circuit, _affect their_ _brightness?_

3

SHORTER

© Chris Jones 2008

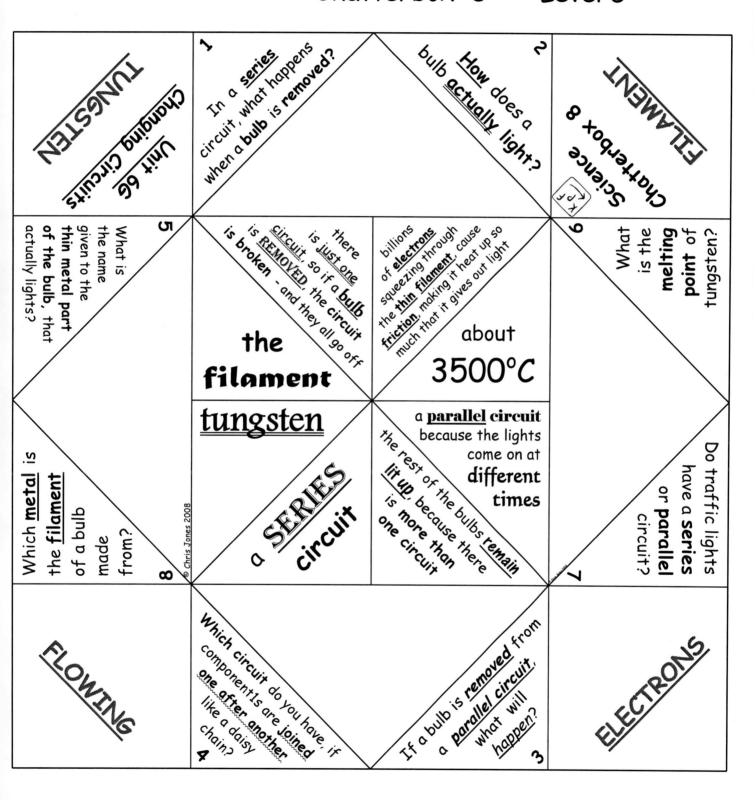

TUNGSTEN

Unit 6G
Changing Circuits

1
In a **series** circuit, what happens when a **bulb** is **removed**?

2
How does a bulb **actually light**?

Science
Chatterbox 8

FILAMENT

5
What is the name given to the **thin metal part of the bulb**, that actually lights?

there is **just one circuit**, so if a **bulb** is **REMOVED**, the **circuit** is **broken** - and they all go off

billions of **electrons** squeezing through the **thin filament**, cause **friction**, making it heat up so much that it gives out light

about
3500°C

6
What is the **melting point of** tungsten?

the
filament

tungsten

a **parallel** circuit because the lights come on at **different times**

the rest of the bulbs **remain lit up**, because there is **more than one circuit**

Do traffic lights have a **series** or **parallel** circuit?

Which **metal** is the **filament** of a bulb made from?

a **SERIES** circuit

© Chris Jones 2008

8

7

FLOWING

Which **circuit** do you have, if components are joined **one after another** like a daisy chain?

4

If a bulb is **removed** from a **parallel circuit**, what will **happen?**

3

ELECTRONS

© Chris Jones 2008

Blank Chatterbox

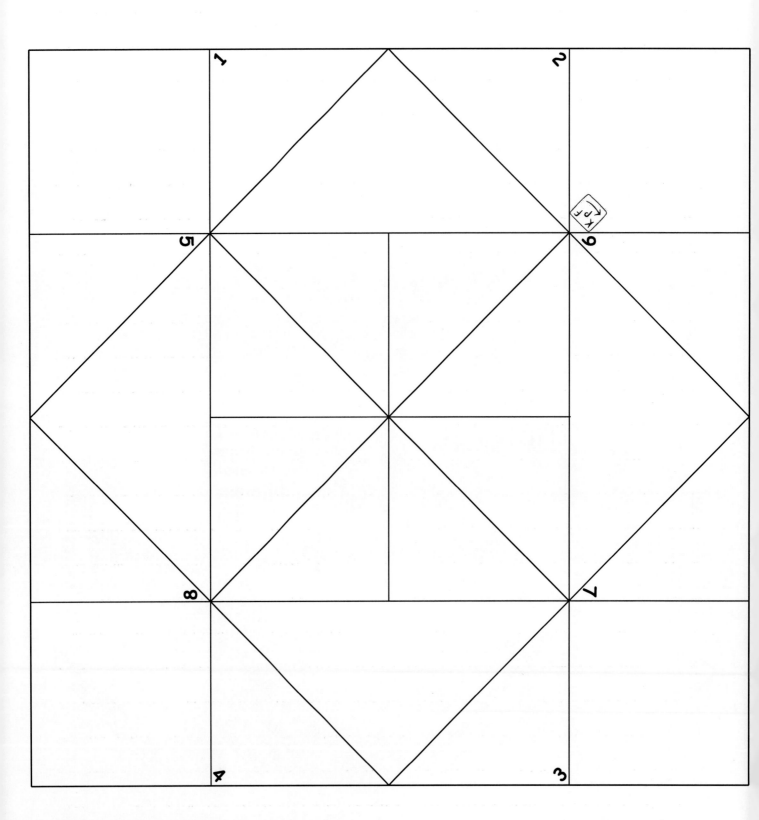

_____

_____

_____

_____

_____

_____

_____

_____

_____

_____

_____

_____

_____

_____

_____

_____

_____

_____

_____

_____

_____